W9-CQG-911

Treat yourself to an hour with Berlitz

Just listen and repeat

It's fun, not work. And you'll surprise your friends and yourself with the speed you pick up some basic expressions in the foreign language of your choice. These cassettes are recorded in hi-fi with four voices. Bringing native speakers into your home, they permit you to polish your accent and learn the basic phrases before you depart.

With each cassette is a helpful 32-page script, containing pronunciation tips and the complete text of the dual-language recording.

An ideal companion for your Berlitz phrase book, pocket dictionary or travel guide. Order now!

BERLITZ SINGLE CASSETTES
Only $9.95/£5.95 (incl. VAT)

Arabic	278 ☐	Italian	223 ☐
Chinese	221 ☐	Japanese	285 ☐
Danish	297 ☐	Norwegian	287 ☐
Dutch	295 ☐	Portuguese	279 ☐
Finnish	296 ☐	Russian	288 ☐
French	219 ☐	Serbo-Croatian	298 ☐
German	220 ☐	Spanish (Castil)	222 ☐
Greek	294 ☐	Spanish (Lat Am)	259 ☐
Hebrew	289 ☐	Swedish	286 ☐

TOTAL SINGLES

Please note the total number of each item requested and complete the reverse side of this order form. **11406**

$	£
From New York Total units _____ at $9.95 each Total amount enclosed $ _____ (N.Y. residents add sales tax)	**From London** Total units _____ at £5.95 Total amount enclosed £ _____ (VAT is included)

Name _____

Address _____

_____

_____

Please complete and return this order form to:

Traveller's
Shopping Service
3490 Lawson Blvd.
Oceanside, N.Y. 11572
U.S.A.

or

Traveller's
Shopping Service
1 St. Anne's Road
Eastbourne
East Sussex, BN21 3UN
U.K.

Please order Berlitz books through your bookseller. Should you encounter any difficulties, write directly to any of the distributors listed on the back cover.

11406

BERLITZ®

NORWEGIAN
FOR TRAVELLERS

By the staff of Editions Berlitz

Library of Congress Catalog Card Number: 75-11283

Revised edition
7th printing 1984

Printed in Switzerland

Berlitz Trademark Reg. U.S. Patent Office
and other countries—Marca Registrada

Editions Berlitz
1, avenue des Jordils
1000 Lausanne 6, Switzerland

Preface

In preparing this complete revision of *Norwegian for Travellers*, we have taken into consideration a wealth of suggestions and criticisms from phrase-book users around the world. As a result, this new edition features:

a) a complete phonetic transcription throughout indicating the pronunciation of all words and phrases you'll need to know on your trip

b) special sections showing the replies your listener might give to you. Just hand him the book and let him point to the appropriate phrase. This is especially practical in certain difficult situations (doctor, garage mechanic, etc.)

c) a complete revision of the section on Eating Out to make it even more useful in a restaurant

d) a tipping chart and a more comprehensive reference section in the back of the book.

These are new features. They complement what has become the world's most popular phrase-book series, helping you with:

* all the phrases and supplementary vocabulary you'll need on your trip

* a wide variety of tourist and travel facts, tips and useful information

* audio aids in the form of cassettes

* quick reference through colour coding. The major features of the contents are on the back cover. A complete index is found inside.

These are just a few of the practical advantages. In addition, the book will prove a valuable introduction to life in Norway.

There's a comprehensive section on Eating Out, giving translations and explanations for practically anything one would find on a Norwegian menu; there's a complete Shopping Guide that will enable you to obtain virtually anything you want.

Trouble with the car? Turn to the mechanic's manual with its dual-language terms. Feeling ill? Our medical section provides the most rapid communication possible between you and the doctor.

To make the most of *Norwegian for Travellers*, we suggest that you start with the "Guide to pronunciation". Then go on to "Some basic expressions". This not only gives you a minimum vocabulary; it helps you to pronounce the language. We're particularly grateful to Mrs. Anne-Marie Gay, Mrs. Tore Pamm and Mr. David Pulman for their help in the preparation of this book and to Dr. T. J. A. Bennett and Mr. Harald Småge, who devised the phonetic transcription. We also wish to thank the Norwegian National Travel Office for its assistance.

We shall be very pleased to receive any comments, criticisms and suggestions that you think may help us in preparing future editions.

Thank you. Have a good trip.

Throughout this book, the symbols illustrated here indicate small sections where phrases have been compiled that your foreign listener might like to say to *you*. If you don't understand him, give him the book and let him point to the phrase in his language. The English translation is just beside it.

Basic grammar

The language

Norway has two official written, mutually comprehensible languages, *bokmål* and *nynorsk*. A traveller in Norway must expect to see both, but *bokmål*—the most common—is used throughout this book.

The Norwegian and English languages are very closely linked and have developed along basically similar lines. In many cases the grammar is reminiscent of English with few word endings and simple verb conjugations. If the existence of three genders seems to complicate matters, remember that most nouns are of common gender, and a mistake here will rarely lead to misunderstanding. Word order is to a large extent the same as in English.

Nouns and articles

Norwegian nouns can be of three genders: common (masculine), feminine or neuter. The majority of feminine nouns, however, can also have common (masculine) forms: for example "a night" is *ei* **natt** in the feminine but *en* **natt** in the common form. To simplify matters, we have chosen in this book to use only the two most frequently used genders, the common and the neuter, but you should be aware of the existence of the feminine.

1. Indefinite article (a/an)

common: *en* **stasjon**   a station
neuter: *et* **hotell**   a hotel

In the *indefinite plural*, both common and neuter nouns take an -**(e)r** ending.

common: **stasjon**er   stations
neuter: **hotell**er   hotels

Exceptions: most one-syllable neuter nouns, which remain unchanged in the plural.

et **hus**   a house
hus   houses

GRAMMAR

2. Definite article (the)

Where we, in English, say "the house", the Norwegians say the equivalent of "house-the", i.e. they tag the definite article onto the end of the noun. Once you get over the initial strangeness of the idea you'll find the system easy to handle.

Common nouns take an **-en** ending, neuter nouns an **-et** ending.

| common: | **stasjon**en | the station |
| neuter: | **hotell**et | the hotel |

Thus, in the *singular*, **en** is associated with common nouns*:

en **bil**   a car   **bil**en   the car

and **et** with neuter nouns:

et **glass**   a glass   **glass**et   the glass

In the *plural*, both common and neuter nouns take an **-(e)ne** ending.

| common: | **stasjon**ene | the stations |
| neuter: | **hotell**ene | the hotels |

There are also a certain number of irregular plurals.

3. Possessives

Possession is shown by adding **-s** to each form of the noun in both singular and plural. *Note:* There is no apostrophe.

en stasjon*s*	a station's
stasjoner*s*	stations'
stasjonen*s*	the station's
stasjonene*s*	the stations'

et hotell*s*	a hotel's
hoteller*s*	hotels'
hotellet*s*	the hotel's
hotellene*s*	the hotels'

Adjectives

In English the adjective remains unchanged. In Norwegian there are two different sets of adjectival endings, indefinite and definite, corresponding to the indefinite and definite forms of the nouns.

*Remember the existence of the feminine (see overleaf): "the night" (common form) is **natt**en, but if used in the feminine it is **natt**a.

Indefinite form of the adjective:

singular : with common nouns, the adjective remains unchanged;

with neuter nouns, the adjective takes a -t ending;

plural: with both common and neuter nouns, the adjective
takes an -e ending in the plural.

	singular		plural	
common	(en) **stor stasjon**	(a) big station	**store stasjon**er	big stations
neuter	(et) **stor**t **hotell**	(a) big hotel	**store hotell**er	big hotels

Definite form of the adjective:

The adjective takes an -e ending everywhere, with both common and neuter nouns, in both singular and plural. However,
in this definite usage, **den** must be placed in front of the adjectives in the case of common nouns, **det** with neuter nouns and
de with any plural.

	singular		plural	
common	*den* **store stasjon**en	*the* big station	*de* **store stasjon**ene	*the* big stations
neuter	*det* **store hotell**et	*the* big hotel	*de* **store hotell**ene	*the* big hotels

This definite ending pattern is also used when the adjective is
preceded by a demonstrative adjective (see below).

Demonstrative adjectives

	common	neuter	plural
this/these	**denne**	**dette**	**disse**
that/those	**den**	**det**	**de**

denne **butikken**   *this* shop   *det* **slottet**   *that* castle

GRAMMAR

Possessive adjectives	common	neuter	plural
my	min	mitt	mine
your (see note below)	din	ditt	dine
our	vår	vårt	våre
his		hans	
her		hennes	
its		dens/dets*	
their		deres	
your (see note below)		Deres	

hennes butikk   her shop   *mitt* glass   my glass

Personal pronouns	subject	object
I	jeg	meg
you (see note below)	du	deg
he	han	ham
she	hun	henne
it	den/det*	den/det*
we	vi	oss
you	dere	dere
they	de	dem
you (see note below)	De	Dem

Note: Like many other languages, Norwegian has two forms for "you": an informal one (**du**) and a formal one (**De**). It used to be very easy: **De** was used for strangers, superiors or elders, **du** with friends and family. However, today the tendency is to use the informal **du** for everybody. In this book, we have preferred to keep the formal and more polite **De** form, so that no visitor can give offence to anybody.

Verbs

Here we are concerned only with the infinitive, present tense and imperative.

The infinitive of Norwegian verbs usually ends in -**e** and is preceded by **å** (corresponding to English "to").

å snakke   to speak   **å stoppe**   to stop

*Use **dens** or **den** if "it" is of common gender and **dets** or **det** if "it" is neuter.

The present tense drops the **å** and adds an -**(e)r** to the infinitive ending. This form remains unchanged for all persons.

jeg snakker   I speak   **han stopper**   he stops

The imperative is the infinitive without the -**e** ending and without the preceding **å**.

snakk !   speak !   **stopp !**   stop !

Here are three useful auxiliary verbs:

	to be	to have	to be able to, can
infinitive	**å være**	**å ha**	**å kunne**
present tense (same form for all persons)	**jeg er**, etc.	**jeg har**, etc.	**jeg kan**, etc.
imperative	**vær !**	**ha !**	—

GRAMMAR

Negatives

Ikke (not) is generally placed immediately after the verb.

Bussen kommer.   The bus is coming.
Bussen kommer *ikke.*   The bus is not coming.

Questions

Questions are formed by inverting the subject and the verb.

Bussen stopper her.   The bus stops here.
Stopper bussen her ?   Does the bus stop here ?

Note: On occasions, particularly in word lists, we have eliminated gender altogether (common v. neuter), and offered one choice. For instance, the English "It is" is translated **Det er** (neuter) when it is equally possible the object is common gender, requiring **Den er**.

Guide to pronunciation

This and the following chapter are intended to make you familiar with our system of phonetic transcription and to help you to get used to the sounds of Norwegian.

As a minimum vocabulary for your trip, we've selected a number of basic words and phrases under the title "Some basic expressions" (pages 16-21).

An outline of the spelling and sounds of Norwegian

You'll find the pronunciation of Norwegian letters and sounds explained below, as well as the symbols we're using for them in the transcriptions. The imitated pronunciation should be read as if it were English except for any special rules set out below. Of course, the sounds of any two languages are never exactly the same; but if you follow carefully the indications supplied here, you'll have no difficulty in reading our transcriptions in such a way as to make yourself understood.

Letters written in bold should be stressed. A bar over part of a word (sh$\overline{u}$r) in our phonetic transcription indicates a long vowel.

Consonants

Letter	Approximate pronunciation	Symbol	Example	
b, d, f, h, m, n, p, t, v	as in English			
g	1) before i, y or ei, like y in yet	y	gi	yee
	2) otherwise, like g in go	g	gate	gaater
hv	like v in view	v	hva	vah
j, gj, hj, lj	like y in yet	y	ja	yah
			hjem	yehm

k	1) before **i**, **y** or **j**, rather like **ch** in Scottish lo**ch**, or even more like **ch** in German i**ch**	kh	**kjær** **kyst**	kh**ǣ**r khewst
	2) otherwise like **k** in **k**it	k	**kaffe**	kahffer
l	always as in lee, never as in bell	l	**salt**	sahlt
r	slightly rolled in the front of the mouth, except in south-western Norway where it is pronounced in the back of the mouth (as in French)	r	**reis**	rayss
rs	generally pronounced like **sh** in **sh**ut in eastern Oslo area, including the Oslo area (elsewhere both letters are pronounced)	sh	**norsk**	noshk
s	always as in **s**o	s/ss	**spansk** **rose**	spahnsk rōōsser
sj, skj, sk	when followed by **i**, **y** or **ø** or **øy**, like **sh** in **sh**ut	sh	**sjø** **ski**	sh**ū**r shee

PRONUNCIATION

1. The letters **c**, **q**, **w**, **z** are only found in foreign words, and tend to be pronounced as in the language of origin.

2. In the groups **rd**, **rl**, **rn** and **rt**, the **r** tends not to be pronounced but influences the pronunciation of the following consonant, which is then pronounced with the tip of the tongue well behind the upper teeth ridge (turned upwards at the front). This "retroflex" pronunciation of **d**, **l**, **n** or **t**, is shown by an **r** placed above the line before the consonant, e.g. *gjerne—*y**ǣ**ʳner.

Vowels

A vowel is generally long in stressed syllables when it's the final letter or followed by only one consonant. If followed by two or more consonants, or in unstressed syllables, the vowel is generally short.

a	1) when long, like **a** in car	aa	**dag**	daag
	2) when short, fairly like **u** in cut or **o** in American doll	ah	**takk**	tahk
e	1) when long, like **ay** in say, but a pure sound, *not* a diphthong	$\overline{ay}$	**se**	$s\overline{ay}$
	2) when short, like **e** in get	eh	**penn**	pehn
	3) when followed by **r**, often like **a** in bad; long or short	$\overline{æ}$ æ	**her** **herr**	h$\overline{æ}$r hærr
	4) when unstressed, like **a** in about	er*	**lese**	l$\overline{ay}$sser
i	1) when long, like **ee** in see, but with the tongue more raised, and the lips more drawn back at the sides	ee	**ti**	tee
	2) when short, between **ea** in heat and **i** in hit	i	**kiste**	khisster
o	1) when long, like **oo** in soon, but with the lips more rounded (when followed by -**rt**, -**st**, -**m** and -**nd**, it may be pronounced short)	$\overline{oo}$ oo	**god** **ost**	g$\overline{oo}$ oost
	2) occasionally, when long, like **aw** in saw	aw	**tog**	tawg
	3) when short, generally like **o** in hot	o	**stoppe**	stopper
u	1) something like the **ew** in few, or Scottish **oo** in good; since it is very close to the Norwegian **y**-sound, we use the same symbol for both; can be long or short	$\overline{ew}$ ew	**mur** **buss**	m$\overline{ew}$r bewss
	2) in some words, like **oo** in foot	oo	**pumpe**	poomper
y	very much like the sound described under **u** (1) above; put your tongue in the position for the **ee** in bee, and then round your lips as for the **oo** in pool	$\overline{ew}$ ew	**by** **stykke**	b$\overline{ew}$ stewkker
æ	1) before **r** like **a** in bad; usually long but sometimes short	$\overline{æ}$ æ	**lære** **lærd**	l$\overline{æ}$rer læ'd

---

* The **r** should not be pronounced when reading this transcription.

	2) otherwise, like **ay** in s**ay** but a pure sound, not a diphthong	$\overline{ay}$	h**æ**l	h$\overline{ay}$l
ø	like **ur** in f**ur** but with the lips rounded and without any **r**-sound; either long or short	$\overline{ur}$ ur	d**ø**r s**ø**tt	d$\overline{ur}$r surt
å	1) when long, like **aw** in s**aw**	aw	p**å**	paw
	2) when short (rare), more like **o** in h**o**t	o	g**å**tt	got

Diphthongs

au	rather like **ow** in n**ow**, though the first part is the Norwegian **ø**-sound	ow	s**au**	sow
ei	like **ay** in s**ay** but often reminiscent of **igh** in s**igh**	ay	g**ei**t	yayt
øy	rather like **oy** in b**oy**, though the first part is the Norwegian **ø**-sound	oy	h**øy**	hoy

Silent letters

1. The letter **g** is generally silent in the endings -**lig** and -**ig**.

2. The letter **d** is generally silent after **l** or **n** or after **r** at the end of a word (with lengthening of the vowel) or often after a long vowel, e.g. ho**ld**e, la**nd**, gå**rd**.

3. The letter **t** is silent in the definite form ("the") of neuter nouns (e.g., eple**t**) and in the pronoun de**t**.

4. The letter **v** is silent in a few words, e.g., sel**v**, tol**v**, hal**v**, søl**v**.

Intonation

In Norwegian, intonation is sometimes used to distinguish between words. Since Norwegians don't expect foreigners to have mastered such subtleties, the tones are not shown in our pronunciation guide.

Some basic expressions

Yes.	**Ja.**	yah
No.	**Nei.**	nay
Please.	**Vennligst.**	**vehn**ligst
Thank you.	**Takk.**	tahk
Thank you very much.	**Tusen takk.**	**tew**ssern tahk
That's all right.	**Ikke noe å takke for.**	ikker **noo**er aw **tahk**ker for
You're welcome.	**Vær så god.**	**vær** saw goo

Greetings

Good morning.	**God morgen.**	goo **maw**ern
Good afternoon.	**God dag.**	goo daag
Good evening.	**God kveld.**	goo kvehl
Good night.	**God natt.**	goo naht
Good-bye.	**Adjø.**	ah**dyur**
See you later.	**På gjensyn.**	paw **yehn**ssewn
This is Mr...	**Dette er herr...**	**deht**ter ær hærr
This is Mrs...	**Dette er fru...**	**deht**ter ær frew
This is Miss...	**Dette er frøken...**	**deht**ter ær **frur**kern
How do you do?	**God dag.***	goo daag
I'm pleased to meet you.	**Det gleder meg å hilse på Dem.**	**day glay**derr may aw **hil**sser paw dehm
How's it going?	**Hvordan går det?**	voo'dahn gawr day
Very well, thanks.	**Takk, bare bra.**	tahk **baar**er braa
And you?	**Og med Dem?**	o may dehm
Excuse me.	**Unnskyld.**	**ewn**shewl
I beg your pardon.	**Unnskyld.**	**ewn**shewl

*Generally people say "God dag", and shake hands, when introduced.

Questions

Where?	**Hvor?**	voor
Where is...?	**Hvor er...?**	voor ǣr
Where are...?	**Hvor er...?**	voor ǣr
When?	**Når?**	nawr
What?	**Hva?**	vah
How?	**Hvordan?**	voo'dahn
How much?	**Hvor mye?**	voor mew̄er
How many?	**Hvor mange?**	voor mahnger
Who?	**Hvem?**	vehm
Why?	**Hvorfor?**	voorfor
Which?	**Hvilket?**	vilkert
What do you call this in Norwegian?	**Hva kaller man dette på norsk?**	vah **kahl**lerr mahn **deht**ter paw noshk
What do you call that in Norwegian?	**Hva kaller man det på norsk?**	vah **kahl**lerr mahn dāy paw noshk
What do you call these in Norwegian?	**Hva kaller man disse på norsk?**	vah **kahl**lerr mahn **diss**er paw noshk
What do you call those in Norwegian?	**Hva kaller man dem på norsk?**	vah **kahl**lerr mahn dehm paw noshk
What does this mean?	**Hva betyr dette?**	vah bertew̄r **deht**ter
What does that mean?	**Hva betyr det?**	vah bertew̄r dāy

Do you speak...?

Do you speak English?	**Snakker De engelsk?**	snahk**kerr** dee **ehng**erlsk
Is there anyone here who speaks...?	**Er det noen som snakker...her?**	ǣr dāy nō̄ern som snahk**kerr**...hǣr
I don't speak (much) Norwegian.	**Jeg snakker ikke (så mye) norsk.**	yay **snahk**kerr **ik**ker (saw mew̄er) noshk
Could you speak more slowly?	**Kunne De snakke litt saktere?**	**kewn**ner dee **snahk**ker lit **sahk**terrer
Could you repeat that?	**Ville De gjenta det?**	**vill**er dee **yehn**tah dāy
Please write it down.	**Vennligst skriv det ned.**	**vehn**ligst skreev dāy nāy(d)

SOME BASIC EXPRESSIONS

English	Norwegian	Pronunciation
Can you translate this for me?	Kunne De oversette dette for meg?	kewnner dee awveri-ssehter dehtter for may
Can you translate that for us?	Kunne De oversette det for oss?	kewnner dee awverr-ssehter day for oss
Please point to the phrase in the book.	Vær så snill å peke på setningen i boken.	vær saw snil aw payker paw sehtningern ee bookern
Just a minute. I'll see if I can find it in this book.	Et øyeblikk. Jeg skal se om jeg kan finne det i denne boken.	eht oyerblik. yay skahl say om yay kahn finner day ee dehnner bookern
I understand.	Jeg forstår.	yay foshtawr
I don't understand.	Jeg forstår ikke.	yay foshtawr ikker
Do you understand?	Forstår De?	foshtawr dee

Can...?

English	Norwegian	Pronunciation
Can I have...?	Kunne jeg få...?	kewnner yay faw
Can we have...?	Kunne vi få...?	kewnner vee faw
Can you show me...?	Kan De vise meg...?	kahn dee veesser may
I can't.	Jeg kan ikke.	yay kahn ikker
Can you tell me...?	Kan De fortelle meg...?	kahn dee fo'tehller may
Can you help me?	Kan De hjelpe meg?	kahn dee yehlper may
Can I help you?	Kan jeg hjelpe Dem?	kahn yay yehlper dehm
Can you direct me to...?	Kan De vise meg veien til...?	kahn dee veesser may vayern til

Wanting

It is too brusque in Norwegian to say "I want". Use the more polite...

English	Norwegian	Pronunciation
I'd like...	Jeg skulle gjerne ha...	yay skewller yæ'ner haa
We'd like...	Vi skulle gjerne ha...	vee skewller yæ'ner haa
What do you want?	Hva ønsker De?	vah urnskerr dee

Give me...

Give it to me.	**Gi meg det.**	yee may da͞y
Bring me...	**Bring meg...**	bring may
Bring it to me.	**Bring meg det.**	bring may da͞y
Show me...	**Vis meg...**	veess may
Show it to me.	**Vis meg det.**	veess may da͞y
I'm looking for...	**Jeg ser etter...**	yay sa͞yr ehtterr
I'm hungry.	**Jeg er sulten.**	yay ǣr sewltern
I'm thirsty.	**Jeg er tørst.**	yay ǣr tursht
I'm tired.	**Jeg er trett.**	yay ǣr treht
I'm lost.	**Jeg har gått meg bort.**	yay haar got may bo't
It's important.	**Det er viktig.**	da͞y ǣr vikti
It's urgent.	**Det haster.**	da͞y hahssterr
Hurry up!	**Skynd Dem!**	shewn dehm

It is /There is...

It is...	**Det er...**	da͞y ǣr
Is it...?	**Er det...?**	ǣr da͞y
It isn't...	**Det er ikke...**	da͞y ǣr ikker
Here it is.	**Vær så god.**	vǣr saw goo
Here they are.	**Vær så god.**	vǣr saw goo
There is/are...	**Det er...**	da͞y ǣr
Is there/Are there...?	**Er det...?**	ǣr da͞y
There isn't/aren't...	**Det er ikke...**	da͞y ǣr ikker
There isn't/aren't any.	**Det er ikke noen.**	da͞y ǣr ikker no͞oern

It's...

big/small	**stor/liten**	sto͞or/leetern
quick/slow	**rask/langsom**	rahsk/lahngsom
early/late	**tidlig/sent**	teeli/sa͞ynt
cheap/expensive	**billig/dyrt**	billi/dew't

near/far	i nærheten/ langt borte	ee nǣrhehtern/ lahngt bo'te
hot/cold	varm/kald	vahrm/kahl
full/empty	full/tom	fewl/tom
easy/difficult	lett/vanskelig	leht/vahnskerli
heavy/light	tung/lett	toong/leht
open/shut	åpen/lukket	awpern/lookert
right/wrong	rett/galt	reht/gaalt
old/new	gammel/ny	gahmmerl/nēw
old/young	gammel/ung	gahmmerl/oong
next/last	neste/siste	nehsster/sisster
beautiful/ugly	vakker/stygg	vahkker/stewg
free (vacant)/occupied	ledig/opptatt	lāydi/optaht
good/bad	god/dårlig	gōō/daw'li
better/worse	bedre/verre	bāydrer/værrer

Quantities

a little/a lot	litt/mye	lit/mēwer
much/many	mye/mange	mēwer/mahnger
more/less	mer/mindre	māyr/mindrer
enough/too	nok/for	nok/for
some/any	noen	nōōern

Prepositions

at	ved	vāy(d)
on	på	paw
in	i	ee
after	etter	ehtterr

before (time)	**før**	furr
before (place)	**foran**	forrahn
to	**til**	til
from	**fra**	fraa
with	**med**	may(d)
without	**uten**	ewtern
inside	**inne**	inner
outside	**ute**	ewter
through	**gjennom**	yehnnom
up/upstairs	**opp/oppe**	op/opper
down/downstairs	**ned/nede**	nay(d)/nayder
toward(s)	**mot**	moot
until	**inntil**	intil
for	**for/til**	for/til
during	**under/i**	ewnnerr/ee

... and a few more useful words

and	**og**	o(g)
or	**eller**	ehllerr
not	**ikke**	ikker
nothing	**ikke noe/ ingenting**	ikker nooer/ ingernting
none	**ingen**	ingern
very	**meget**	maygert
too (also)	**også**	awssaw
soon	**snart**	snah't
perhaps	**kanskje**	kahnsher
here/there	**her/der**	hæær/dæær
now/then	**nå/da**	naw/daa

Arrival

You've arrived. Whether you've come by ship or plane, you'll have to go through passport and customs formalities. (For car/border control, see page 146.)

There's certain to be somebody around who speaks English. That's why we're making this a brief section. What you really want is to be off to your hotel in the shortest possible time. And here are the steps to get these formalities out of the way quickly.

Passport control

Here's my passport.	**Her er mitt pass.**	hǣr ǣr mitt pahss
I'll be staying...	**Jeg skal være her...**	yay skahl vǣrer hǣr
a few days	**et par dager**	eht paar daagerr
a week	**en uke**	ehn ēwker
two weeks	**to uker**	too ēwkerr
a month	**en måned**	ehn mawnerd
I don't know yet.	**Jeg vet ikke ennå.**	yay vāyt ikker ehnaw
I'm here on holiday.	**Jeg er her på ferie.**	yay ǣr hǣr paw fāyreeer
I'm here on business.	**Jeg er her i forret-ninger.**	yay ǣr hǣr ee forreht-ningerr
I'm just passing through.	**Jeg er bare på gjennomreise.**	yay ǣr baarer paw yehnnomraysser

If the going gets tough:

| I'm sorry, I don't understand. | **Jeg beklager, men jeg forstår ikke.** | yay berklaager, mehn yay foshtawr ikker |
| Is there anyone here who speaks English? | **Er det noen her som snakker engelsk?** | ǣr deh nōōern hǣr som snahkkerr ehngerlsk |

Customs

The chart below shows you what you can bring in duty free
(the allowances in parentheses are for non-European resi-
dents).*

Cigarettes	Cigars	Tobacco	Spirits	Wine
200	250 g.	250 g.	1 l. and 1 l.	
or	or	or	or	
(400)	(500 g.)	(500 g.)	1 l. or 2 l.	

The main airport of Norway, Fornebu, is just outside Oslo.
By international standards it is small and uncomplicated; you
are unlikely to get lost between customs and your taxi. The
customs officer will ask whether you have anything to
declare. If you confess to carrying more than your quota of
tobacco or spirits you'll be asked to pay duty. If you have
nothing to declare, you are likely to be waved through
without inspection. But be honest, because spot checks do
occur.

ARRIVAL

I've nothing to declare.	**Jeg har ingenting å fortolle.**	yay haar **inger**nting aw fo**'tol**ler
I've a...	**Jeg har en...**	yay haar ehn
carton of cigarettes	**kartong sigaretter**	kah**'tong** siggah**reht**terr
bottle of whisky	**flaske whisky**	**flahss**ker ''whisky''
bottle of wine	**flaske vin**	**flahss**ker veen
Must I pay on this?	**Må jeg betale for denne?**	maw yay ber**taal**er for **dehn**ner
How much?	**Hvor mye?**	voor **mew**er
It's for my personal use.	**Det er til eget bruk.**	day ǣr til **ayg**eht brewk
It's not new.	**Den er ikke ny.**	dehn ǣr **ik**ker new

*All allowances are subject to change without notice.

24

ARRIVAL

 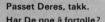

Passet Deres, takk.	Your passport, please.
Har De noe å fortolle?	Have you anything to declare?
Vil De åpne denne bagen?	Please open this bag.
De må betale toll for dette/denne.	You'll have to pay duty on this.
Har De noe mere bagasje?	Have you any more luggage?

Baggage—Porters

Porters may be hard to find at the Oslo airport or the railway station. But you can use the trolleys provided for moving your luggage. Some of the carts have seats for small children.

Are there any porters here/at this station?	Finnes det bærere her/på denne stasjonen?	finners day bærrerer hær/paw dehnner stahshōōnern
Porter!	Bærer!	bærerr
Please take these bags.	Kan De ta denne bagasjen?	kahn dee taa dehnner bahgaashern
That's mine.	Den er min.	dehn ær meen
That's my...	Det er min...	day ær meen
bag/luggage/suitcase	bag/bagasje/koffert	bæg/bahgaasher/kooffeh't
That...one.	Den...	dehn
big/small	store/lille	stōōrer/liller
blue/brown	blå/brune	blaw/brēwner
black/plaid	svarte/rutete	svah'ter/rewtehter
There's one piece missing.	Det mangler en.	day mahnglerr āyn
Take these bags to the...	Kan De ta disse til...?	kahn dee taa disser til
bus	bussen	bewssern
luggage lockers	oppbevaringsboksene	opbehvaaringssbokserner
taxi	drosjen	droshern
How much is that?	Hvor mye koster det?	voor mēwer kossterr dāy

Changing money

If the bank at the airport is closed you'll probably be able to change some money at your hotel.

Full details about money and currency exchange are given on page 134.

Where's the nearest currency exchange office?	**Hvor er nærmeste vekslingskontor?**	voor ær nærmehsster vehkslingsskoontōōr
Can you change these traveller's cheques?	**Kan De veksle disse reisesjekkene?**	kahn dee vehksler disser rayssershehkerner
I want to change some...	**Jeg vil gjerne veksle noen...**	yay vil yǽ'ner vehksler nōōern
dollars	**dollar**	dollahr
pounds	**pund**	pewn
Can you change this into Norwegian crowns?	**Kan De veksle dette til norske kroner?**	kahn dee vehksler dehtter til noshker krōōnerr
What's the exchange rate?	**Hva er kursen?**	vah ær kēwshern

Directions

How do I get to...?	**Hvordan kommer jeg til...?**	voo'dahn kommerr yay til
Where's the bus into town?	**Hvor går bussen inn til byen?**	voor gawr bewssern in til bēwern
Where can I get a taxi?	**Hvor kan jeg få tak i en drosje?**	voor kahn yay faw taak ee ehn drosher
Where can I rent a car?	**Hvor kan jeg leie en bil?**	voor kahn yay layer ehn beel

Hotel reservations

During the summer season it's essential to reserve hotel space in the main cities well in advance. The same situation holds for winter-resort hotels at Christmas and Easter. However, along the roads of Norway there should be no problem finding accommodation in motels, small hotels or boarding houses or in cabins near camping sites. For reservations in northern Norway, telephone ahead.

FOR NUMBERS, see page 175

ARRIVAL

Car rental

There are car rental firms at most airports and terminals and some member of the staff will usually speak English. However, if nobody does, try one of the following:

I'd like a...	**Jeg vil gjerne leie en...**	yay vil y**ǣ**'ner **lay**er ehn
car	**bil**	beel
small car	**liten bil**	**lee**tern beel
large car	**stor bil**	st**oo**r beel
sports car	**sportsbil**	**spoorts**beel
I'd like it for...	**Jeg vil gjerne leie den for...**	yay vil y**ǣ**'ner **lay**er dehn for
a day/4 days	**en dag/4 dager**	ehn daag/4 **daa**gerr
a week/2 weeks	**en uke/2 uker**	ehn **ew**ker/2 **ew**kerr
What's the charge per...	**Hva koster det pr...**	vah **koss**terr d**ay** pær
day	**dag**	daag
week	**uke**	**ew**ker
Does that include mileage?	**Er kilometerprisen inkludert?**	**ǣ**r **khee**loom**ay**terrpreessern inklew**day**'t
What's the charge per kilometre?	**Hva koster det pr. kilometer?**	vah **koss**terr d**ay** pær **khee**loom**ay**terr
Is petrol (gasoline) included?	**Er bensin inkludert?**	**ǣ**r behn**sseen** inklew**day**'t
I want full insurance.	**Jeg vil ha full forsikring.**	yay vil haa fewl forss**ik**ring
I'll be doing about 100 kilometres.	**Jeg kommer til å kjøre ca. 100 km.**	yay **kom**merr til aw kh**ur**rer **seer**kah 100 **khee**loom**ay**terr
What's the deposit?	**Hva er depositumet?**	vah **ǣ**r d**ay**poo**ss**itewmert
I've a credit card.	**Jeg har et kredittkort.**	yay haar eht kreh**dit**ko't
Here's my driving licence.	**Her er sertifikatet mitt.**	h**ǣ**r **ǣ**r sehrtifi**kaa**ter mit

Note: Your own driving licence is valid in Norway. But if you're planning to drive in other countries you may need an international licence.

FOR SIGHTSEEING, see page 75

ARRIVAL

Taxi

All taxis have meters, but it's advisable to ask the approximate fare beforehand. For some trips (for instance, from the airport to town) there may be a fixed rate. This will be posted at the airport.

In principle, the tip is included in the fare in Norway. Nevertheless, your taxi driver won't be offended if you offer him an extra crown or two. On the contrary...

Where can I get a taxi?	**Hvor kan jeg få tak i en drosje?**	voor kahn yay faw taak ee ehn **drosher**
Please get me a cab.	**Vil De vennligst skaffe meg en drosje?**	vil dee **vehn**ligst **skahf**fer may ehn **drosher**
What's the fare to...?	**Hva koster det til...?**	vah **koss**terr dāȳ til
How far is it to...?	**Hvor langt er det til...?**	voor lahngt ǣr dāȳ til
Take me to...	**Jeg skal til...**	yay skahl til
this address	**denne adressen**	**dehn**ner ah**drehss**ern
the town centre	**sentrum i byen**	**sehn**trewm ee **bēēw**ern
the...Hotel	**hotell...**	hoo**tehl**
Turn...at the next corner.	**Kjør til... ved neste kryss.**	khūrr til... vāȳ **nehss**ter krewss
left	**venstre**	**vehn**sstrer
right	**høyre**	**hoy**rer
Go straight ahead.	**Kjør rett frem.**	khūrr rehtt frehm
Stop here, please.	**Kan De stoppe her?**	kahn dee **stopp**er hǣr
I'm in a hurry.	**Jeg har dårlig tid.**	yay haar **daw'**li teed
Could you drive more slowly?	**Vil De kjøre litt saktere?**	vil dee **khū**rrer lit **sahk**tehrer
Could you help me to carry my bags?	**Kunne De hjelpe meg å bære koffertene mine?**	**kewn**ner dee **yehl**per may aw **bǣ**rer **koof**fer'tehner **mee**ner

ARRIVAL

FOR TIPPING, see inside back-cover

Hotel—Other accommodation

Norwegian hotels maintain high standards of comfort and cleanliness. You can get an up-to-date price list of all Norwegian hotels from the Norway Travel Association.

In major tourist centres it's essential to book in advance—and to have your reservation confirmed—during the height of the season. If you're stranded, many towns have a Tourist Information Office.

Although there is no official rating system, there are different classes of accommodation:

Hotell (hoo**tehl**)	In the bigger towns you will find a number of first-class and some de-luxe hotels. Facilities—and prices—cover a wide range, but standards are always high.
Turisthotell (tew**rist**hootehl)	Only the best resort hotels are entitled to be called "tourist" hotels. These establishments are often located near the fjords, mountains and scenic valleys.
Høyfjellshotell (**hoy**fyehlss- hootehl)	Of the same high standard as the *turisthotell*s, these are always located in the mountains.
Hospits (hoo**spits**)	A boarding-house or hostel, too small to be classed as a hotel (though they have many of the same facilities). Some are owned by organizations such as the YMCA and YWCA.
Turiststasjon (tew**rist**stah- shōōn)	An unpretentious establishment with comfortable, scrupulously clean rooms. There's generally a cosy lounge with an open hearth. You can count on good wholesome food.
Fjellstue (**fyell**stēwer)	A mountain inn, very similar to a *turist-stasjon*.
Turisthytte (tew**rist**hewtter)	A tourist hut, often located in a remote, hard-to-reach spot. Most bedrooms are for 4 to 6 persons, with few singles or doubles.

Ungdoms-	A youth hostel. With the exception of those
herberge	located in skiing country, most of Norway's
(**oong**doms-	140 youth hostels are open only in summer.
hǣrbærger)	

Utleiehytte	A chalet that can be rented for a period of
(**ēwt**layer-	time in summer or winter. Most are located in
hewtter)	picturesque settings.

In this section, we're mainly concerned with the smaller and medium-priced hotels and boarding houses. You'll have no language difficulties in the luxury and first-class hotels where most of the staff speak English.

In the next few pages we consider your requirements—step by step—from arrival to departure. You needn't read all of it; just turn to the situation that applies.

Checking in—Reception

My name is...	**Mitt navn er...**	mit navn ǣr
I've a reservation.	**Jeg har bestilt.**	yay haar berstilt
We've reserved two rooms, a single and a double.	**Vi har reservert to værelser, et enkelt og et dobbelt.**	vee haar rāysærvāy't too vǣrerlsserr, eht ehnkerlt o eht **dobb**erlt
I wrote to you last month.	**Jeg skrev til Dem i forrige måned.**	yay skrāyv til dehm ee **forr**eeer **maw**nerd
Here's the confirmation.	**Her er bekreftelsen.**	hǣr ǣr ber**krehf**terlssern
I'd like...	**Jeg vil gjerne ha...**	yay vil yǣ'ner haa
a single room	**et enkeltrom**	eht **ehnk**erlt-room
a double room	**et dobbeltrom**	eht **dobb**erlt-room
two single rooms	**to enkeltrom**	too **ehnk**erlt-room
a room with twin beds	**et rom med dobbelt-seng**	eht room māy **dobb**erlt-sehng
a room with a bath	**et rom med bad**	eht room māy baad
a room with a shower	**et rom med dusj**	eht room māy dewsh
a room with a balcony	**et rom med balkong**	eht room māy bahlkong
a room with a view	**et rom med utsikt**	eht room māy **ēwt**sikt
a suite	**en suite**	ehn **svee**ter

HOTEL

We'd like a room...	Vi vil gjerne ha et rom...	vee vil yǣ'rner haa eht room
in the front	på forsiden	paw forseedern
at the back	på baksiden	paw baakseedern
facing the sea	mot sjøen	moot shūrern
facing the courtyard	mot gårdsplassen	moot gawrssplahssern
It must be quiet.	Det må være rolig.	day maw vǣrer rooli
Is there...?	Er det...?	ǣr day
air conditioning	luftventilasjon	lewftvehntilahshoon
heating	oppvarming	opvahrming
a radio/a television in the room	radio/fjernsyn på rommet	raadio/fyǣ'nssewn paw roommer
a laundry service	vaskeri	vahskerree
room service	romservice	roomsehrviss
hot water	varmt vann	vahrmt vahn
running water	rennende vann	rehnernder vahn
a private toilet	eget toalett	ǣgert tooahleht

How much?

What's the price...?	Hva koster det...?	vah kossterr day
per week	pr. uke	pær ēwker
per night	pr. natt	pær naht
for bed and breakfast	for overnatting og frokost	for awverrnahting o frookosst
excluding meals	uten måltider	ēwtern mawlteederr
for full board	med full pensjon	māy fewl pehnshoon
for half board	med halvpensjon	māy hahlpehnshoon
Does that include...?	Inkluderer det...?	inklewdāyrerr day
breakfast	frokost	frookosst
meals	måltider	mawlteederr
service	service	sehrviss
tax	avgift	ahvyift
Is there any reduction for children?	Er det reduksjon for barn?	ǣr day rāydewkshoon for baa'n
Do you charge for the baby?	Koster det noe for babyen?	kossterr day nooer for bāybeeern
That's too expensive.	Det er for dyrt.	day ǣr for dew't
Haven't you anything cheaper?	Har De noe rimeligere?	haar dee nooer reemerleeerrerr

FOR NUMBERS, see page 175

How long?

We'll be staying...	Vi blir...	vee bleer
overnight only	bare natten over	baarer nahttern awverr
a few days	noen få dager	nōōen faw daagerr
a week (at least)	en uke (minst)	ehn ēwker (minst)
I don't know yet.	Jeg vet ikke ennå.	yay vāyt ikker ehnnaw

Decision

May I see the room?	Kan jeg få se værelset?	kahn yay faw sāy vǣrerlsser
No, I don't like it.	Nei, jeg liker det ikke.	nay, yay leekerr dāy ikker
It's too...	Det er for...	dāy ǣr for
cold	kaldt	kahlt
hot	varmt	vahrmt
dark	mørkt	murrkt
small	lite	leeter
noisy	mye bråk	mēwer brawk
I asked for a room with a bath.	Jeg ba om et værelse med bad.	yay baa om eht vǣrerlsser māy baad
Do you have anything...?	Har De noe...?	haar dee nōōer
better	bedre	bāydrer
bigger	større	sturrer
cheaper	billigere	billeeerrer
quieter	roligere	rōōleeerrer
higher up	høyere opp	hoyerrer op
lower down	lenger nede	lehngerr nāyder
Do you have a room with a better view?	Har De et rom med bedre utsikt?	haar dee eht room māy bāydrer ēwtsikt
That's fine. I'll take it.	Det er bra. Jeg tar det.	dāy ǣr braa. yay taar dāy

Bills

These are usually paid weekly or upon departure if you stay less than a week. Most hotels offer a reduction of 50 per cent for children under twelve.

FOR DAYS OF THE WEEK, see page 181

HOTEL

Tipping

At hotels, service (10-15 %) is included in the price or is added to the bill. Thus there is no need to tip anyone in the hotel except for special services. See our suggestions inside the back cover.

Registration

Upon arrival at a hotel or boarding-house you'll be asked to fill in a registration form (*skjema for utlendinger*—**shay**mah for **ewt**lehningerr), giving your name, home address, passport number and further destination. It's almost certain to carry an English translation. If it doesn't, ask the desk-clerk:

What does this mean?	**Hva betyr dette?**	vah ber**tewr** deh**t**ter

The desk-clerk will probably ask you for your passport. He may want to keep it for a while, even overnight. Don't worry. You'll get it back. He may want to ask you the following questions:

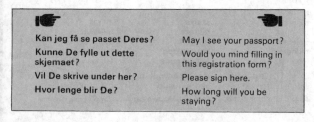

Kan jeg få se passet Deres?	May I see your passport?
Kunne De fylle ut dette skjemaet?	Would you mind filling in this registration form?
Vil De skrive under her?	Please sign here.
Hvor lenge blir De?	How long will you be staying?

What's my room number?	**Hva er værelse-nummeret mitt?**	vah **ær** v**æ**rerlsser-**noom**mehrer mit
Will you have our bags sent up?	**Kan De sende opp bagasjen vår?**	kahn dee **sehn**ner op bah**gaa**shern vawr

HOTEL

Service, please

bellboy	**pikkoloen**	pikkolooern
maid	**stuepiken**	st$\overline{ew}$erpeekern
manager	**direktøren**	direhkt$\overline{ur}$rern
room service	**romservice**	roomsehrviss
switchboard operator	**sentralbordbe-tjeningen**	sehntraalb$\overline{oo}$rbeh-ty$\overline{ay}$ningern
waiter	**kelneren**	kehlnerrern
waitress	**serveringsdamen**	særv$\overline{ay}$ringssdaamern

When actually addressing restaurant personnel, call the waiter *kelner* (**kehl**nerr) and the waitress *frøken* (**fr$\overline{ur}$**kern).

General requirements

Please ask the maid to come up.	**Vil De be stuepiken komme opp?**	vil dee b$\overline{ay}$ st$\overline{ew}$erpeekern **kom**mer op
Who is it?	**Hvem er det?**	vehm $\overline{æ}$r d$\overline{ay}$
Just a minute.	**Et øyeblikk!**	eht oyerblik
Is there a bath on this floor?	**Finnes det et bad i denne etasjen?**	finnerss d$\overline{ay}$ eht baad ee dehnner ehtaashern
How does this shower work?	**Hvordan virker denne dusjen?**	voo'dahn veerkerr **dehnner** dewshern
Where's the plug for the razor?	**Hvor er stikkontakten for barbermaskinen?**	voor $\overline{æ}$r stikkontahktern for bahrb$\overline{ay}$rmahsheenern
What's the voltage here?	**Hvilken spenning er det her?**	vilkern **spehn**ning $\overline{æ}$r d$\overline{ay}$ h$\overline{æ}$r
Can we have breakfast in our room?	**Kan vi få servert fro-kost på rommet?**	kahn vee faw særv$\overline{ay}$'t fr$\overline{oo}$-kosst paw **room**mer
I'd like to leave these in your safe.	**Jeg vil gjerne legge fra meg dette i safen.**	yay vil y$\overline{æ}$'ner lehgger fraa may **deh**tter ee sayfern
Can you find me a baby-sitter?	**Kan De skaffe meg en barnevakt?**	kahn dee **skahf**fer may ehn **baa'**nervahkt

RING ETTER ROMSERVICE
RING FOR SERVICE

34

May I have a/an/some...?	Kan jeg få...?	kahn yay faw
ashtray	et askebeger	eht **ahs**kerbāygerr
bath towel	et badehåndkle	eht **baa**derhawnklāy
extra blanket	et ekstra teppe	eht **ehk**strah **teh**pper
duvet	en dyne	ehn **dēw**ner
envelopes	noen konvolutter	**nōō**ern konvoo**lewt**terr
(more) hangers	noen (flere) hengere	**nōō**ern (**flāy**rer) **heh**ngerrer
extra pillow	en ekstra pute	ehn **ehk**strah **pēw**ter
reading lamp	en leselampe	ehn **lāy**sserlahmper
soap	en såpe	ehn **saw**per
writing paper	noe skrivepapir	**nōō**er **skree**verpahpeer
Where's the...?	Hvor er...?	voor **ǣr**
barber's	herrefrisøren	hærrerfriss**ūū**rrern
bathroom	badet	**baa**der
dining-room	spisesalen	**spees**serssaalern
hairdresser's	frisørsalongen	friss**ūū**rssahlongern
restaurant	restauranten	rehsterr**rahng**ern
television room	fjernsynsrommet	fy**ǣ**'nssewnssroomer
toilet	toalettet	tooah**leht**ter

Breakfast

At most hotels you can get a continental breakfast consisting of coffee or tea, bread, butter and jam, as well as fruit juice. But the real Norwegian breakfast (*frokost*—**frōō**kosst) is a more substantial meal. You have a choice of hot or cold cereals, several types of bread, herring and sardines, cold meat and salads, cheeses, jams, eggs, milk and coffee.

I'll have a/an/some...	Jeg vil gjerne ha...	yay vil y**ǣ**'ner haa
bacon and eggs	bacon og egg	**bay**kern o ehg
cereals (hot)	grøt	grūrt
cereals (cold)	cornflakes	**korn**flayks
eggs	egg	ehg
boiled egg	kokt egg	kookt ehg
soft/hard/medium	bløtkokt/hårdkokt/middels kokt	**blūt**kookt/**hawr**kookt/**mid**derls kookt
fried eggs	stekte egg	**stehk**ter ehg
poached eggs	forlorne egg	fo'**lōōr**ner ehg
scrambled eggs	eggerøre	**ehg**gerrūrrer

fruit juice	fruktsaft	frewktssahft
grapefruit	grapefrukt	gräypfrewkt
orange	appelsin	ahperlsseen
pineapple	ananas	ahnahnahss
tomato	tomat	toommaat
ham and eggs	skinke og egg	shinker o ehg
jam	syltetøy	sewltertoy
marmalade	marmelade	mahrmerlaader
omelet	omelett	oomerleht
pancakes	pannekaker	pahnnerkaakerr
(pork) sausages	(svine)pølser	(sveener)purlsserr
porridge	grøt	grürt
toast	ristet brød	risstert brür
yoghurt	youghurt	yōōgew't
May I have some...?	Kan jeg få litt...?	kahn yay faw lit
hot/cold milk	varm/kald melk	vahrm/kahl mehlk
cream/sugar	fløte/sukker	flürter/sookkerr
bread/rolls	brød/rundstykker	brür/rewnsstewkkerr
butter	smør	smurr
salt/pepper	salt/pepper	sahlt/pehpperr
coffee/tea	kaffe/te	kahffer/teh
hot chocolate	varm sjokolade	vahrm shookoolaader
lemon/honey	sitron/honning	sitrōōn/honning
hot water	varmt vann	vahrmt vahn
Could you bring me a...?	Kan De gi meg...?	kahn dee yee may
cup	en kopp	ehn kop
fork	en gaffel	ehn gahfferl
glass	et glass	eht glahss
knife	en kniv	ehn kneev
napkin	en serviett	ehn særvyeht
plate	en tallerken	ehn tahlærkern
spoon	en skje	ehn shāy

HOTEL SERVICE

Difficulties

The...doesn't work.	...er ikke i orden.	ær ikker ee ordern
air-conditioner	luftventilasjonen	lewftvehntilahshōōnern
fan	viften	viftern
heating	sentralvarmen	sehntraalvahrmern
light	lyset	lēwsser
radio	radioen	raadioern
tap	vannkranen	vahnkraanern
toilet	toalettet	tooahlehtter
ventilator	ventilasjonsanlegget	vehntilahshōōnsssahnlehgger

FOR EATING OUT, see pages 38-64

The wash-basin is clogged.	Vasken er tett.	vahsskern ær teht
The window is jammed.	Vinduet sitter fast.	vindewer sitterr fahsst
The blind is stuck.	Rullegardinet sitter fast.	rewllergah'deener sitterr fahsst
I can't open the wardrobe.	Garderobeskapet lar seg ikke åpne.	gahrderōōbersskaaper laar say ikker awpner
The door won't lock.	Døren kan ikke lukkes.	dūrrern kahn ikker lookkerss
These aren't my shoes.	Dette er ikke mine sko.	dehtter ær ikker meener skōō
This isn't my laundry.	Dette er ikke mitt tøy.	dehtter ær ikker mit toy
There's no hot water.	Det er ikke varmt vann.	dāy ær ikker vahrmt vahn
I've left my key in my room.	Jeg har glemt nøkkelen på rommet.	yay hahr glehmt nurkkerlern paw roommer
The bulb is burnt out.	Lyspæren er gått.	lewsspærern ær got
The...is broken.	...virker ikke.	virkerr ikker
lamp	lampen	lahmpern
plug	stikkontakten	stikkoontahktern
shutter	vinduslemmen	vindewsslehmmern
switch	bryteren	brewterrern
venetian blind	persiennen	pæshiehnnern
window shade	rullegardinet	rewlergaa'deener
Can you get it repaired?	Kan De reparere det?	kahn dee rehpahrāyrer dāy

Telephone—Mail—Callers

Can you get me Oslo 24 35 67?	Kan De få forbindelse med Oslo 24 35 67?	kahn dee faw forbinnerlsser māy oossloo 24 35 67
Do you have any stamps?	Har De frimerker?	haar dee freemærkerr
Would you please mail this for me?	Kan De poste dette for meg?	kahn dee posster dehtter for may
Are there any messages for me?	Er det noen beskjed til meg?	ær dāy nōōern bershāy til may

FOR POST OFFICE and TELEPHONE, see page 137-141

Checking out

May I please have my bill?	**Kan jeg få regningen?**	kahn yay faw **ray**ningern
I'm leaving early tomorrow. Please have my bill ready.	**Jeg reiser i morgen tidlig. Kan De ha regningen klar?**	yay **rays**serr ee **maw**ern **tee**li. kahn dee ha **ray**ningern klaar
We'll be checking out around noon/soon.	**Vi reiser ca. kl. 12/ snart.**	vee **rays**serr **seer**kah **klok**kern tol/snaa't
When is check-out time?	**Hvilket klokkeslett må vi være ute av rommet?**	**vil**kert **klok**kerssleht maw vee **væ**rer **ew**ter ahv **room**mer
I must leave at once.	**Jeg må reise med en gang.**	yay maw **rays**ser māy ehn gahng
Is everything included?	**Er alt inkludert?**	ār ahlt inklew**day**'t
You've made a mistake in this bill, I think.	**Jeg tror De har gjort en feil på regningen.**	yay trōōr dee hahr yoort ehn fayl paw **ray**ningern
Can you get us a taxi?	**Kan De få tak i en drosje til oss?**	kahn dee faw taak ee ehn **dro**sher til oss
When's the next... to Bergen?	**Når går neste... til Bergen?**	nawr gawr **nehs**ster... til **bær**gern
bus	**buss**	bewss
train	**tog**	tawg
plane	**fly**	flew
Would you send someone to bring down my baggage?	**Vil De sende noen til å bære ned bagasjen min?**	vil dee **sehn**ner **nōō**ern til aw **bæ**rer nāy bah**gaa**shern meen
We're in a great hurry.	**Vi har veldig dårlig tid.**	vee hahr **vehl**di **daw'**li teed
Here's my/our forwarding address.	**Her er min/vår neste adresse.**	hær ār meen/vawr **nehs**ster ah**drehs**ser
You have my home address.	**De har min hjemme-adresse.**	dee hahr meen **yehm**mer-ah**drehs**ser
It's been a very enjoyable stay.	**Det har vært et meget hyggelig opphold.**	dāy hahr væ't eht **māy**gert **hewg**gerli **op**hol
I hope we'll come again sometime.	**Jeg håper vi kommer tilbake hit engang.**	yay **haw**perr vee **kom**merr til**baa**ker heet ehn**gahng**

HOTEL SERVICE

FOR TAXI, see page 27

Eating out

Norway offers a wide selection of places to eat, but fewer for drinking.

Restaurant
(rehster**rahng**)

In the major cities there is an excellent choice of restaurants serving Norwegian specialities. The menu (*spisekartet*—**spees**serkah'ter) is often displayed in the window or just outside.

Norwegian specialities emphasize seafood—lobster, salmon, cod, flounder and trout.

Licensing restrictions permit only the major restaurants and hotels in the towns —and "mountain" and "tourist" hotels in the countryside— to serve spirits (liquor).

Kafeteria
(kahfer**tāy**riah)

Usually self-service, these inexpensive eating places provide simple meals. The Norwegians have also adopted the term *snackbar*. Usually you must buy food to obtain wine or even beer.

Kafé
(kah**fāy**)

Bakeries often host coffee shops as well. Here you may have coffee or tea along with a slice of cake or a sandwich. A *kaffebar* (**kahf**ferbaar) is similar, but only pastries and ice-cream are served.

Kro
(kr**oo**)

Usually simple cafeteria-restaurants found on main roads. They are inexpensive self-service establishments.

Steakhouse (**stayk**howss)	Not surprisingly, the fare tends toward T-bones.
Grillrestaurant (grilrehster**rahng**)	The main dishes here are grilled fish, lamb or chicken.
Pub—Bar (purb—baar)	Pubs and bars are scarce in Norway. Wherever you are able to find it, Norwegian beer is recommended (see page 62)

Meal times and eating habits

Generally, breakfast is served between 8 and 10 a.m. (see page 34 for a breakfast menu).

Dinner (*middag*—**mid**daag) is the main meal of the day. At cafés and modest hotels it's usually served between 2 and 5 p.m. If you can't wait that long, look for the special sandwich buffets which operate from 11 a.m. to 1 p.m. At larger hotels a smaller lunch or a cold buffet (*koldtbord*—**kolt**bōōr) is offered (see page 47). This is a more ample version of the typical Norwegian breakfast and also includes hot dishes in spite of its name.

At large hotels and better restaurants, dinner is served starting about 7 p.m.

In addition to à-la-carte items, one or more set menus (*dagens rett*—**daa**gehnss reht) may be listed. The service charge is always included in the bill. Tipping is up to you: small change after a snack, perhaps an extra five or ten per cent after a really good meal.

FOR BREAKFAST, see page 34

Hungry

I'm hungry.	**Jeg er sulten.**	yay **ær** sewltern
I'm thirsty.	**Jeg er tørst.**	yay **ær** tursht
Can you recommend a good restaurant?	**Kan De anbefale en god restaurant?**	kahn dee **ahn**berfaaler ehn gōō rehsterr**rahng**
Are there any good, cheap restaurants around here?	**Finnes det noen gode, billige restauranter her?**	finnerss dāy nōōern gōōer billeeer rehsterrahngerr hǣr
I'd like to reserve a table for 4.	**Jeg vil gjerne bestille et bord til 4.**	yay vil **yǣ**'ner berstiller eht bōōr til 4
We'll come at 8 o'clock.	**Vi kommer klokken 8.**	vee kommerr klokkern 8

A timely word of warning before you even set off for your restaurant. Throughout the Scandinavian countries driving after drinking is a serious offence. A single glass of beer or wine will cost you your driving licence if you're involved in an accident.

Even without an accident, the consumption of as few as two small glasses of beer might infringe the law. There is no special dispensation for foreign tourists...

To play safe, follow Norwegian practice: make sure the driver sticks to soft drinks, take a taxi or walk.

Asking and ordering

Good evening. I'd like a table for 3.	**God aften. Jeg vil gjerne ha et bord til 3.**	gōō **ahf**tern. yay vil **yǣ**'ner haa eht bōōr til 3
Could we have a table...?	**Kan vi få et bord...?**	kahn vee faw eht bōōr
in the corner	**i hjørnet**	ee **yūr**'ner
by the window	**ved vinduet**	vāy vindewer
outside	**utenfor**	**ēw**ternfor
on the terrace	**på terrassen**	paw teh**rahss**ern

EATING OUT

May I please have the menu?	**Kan De gi meg spisekartet?**	kahn dee yee may **speess**erkah'ter
What's this?	**Hva er dette?**	vah **ǣr deht**ter
Do you have...?	**Har De...?**	haar dee
a set menu	**dagens rett**	**daa**gernss reht
local dishes	**lokal spesialitet**	look**aal** spehssyahlit**ayt**
a children's menu	**barnemeny**	baa'nermehn**ew**

Hva ønsker De?	What would you like?
Jeg anbefaler dette.	I recommend this.
Hva ønsker De å drikke?	What would you like to drink?
Vi har ikke...	We haven't got...
Ønsker De...?	Do you want...?

EATING OUT

I'd like...	**Jeg vil gjerne ha...**	yay vil y**ǣ**'ner haa
Is service included?	**Er service inkludert?**	**ǣr sehr**viss inklew**day't**
Could we have a/an ...please?	**Kan vi få...**	kahn vee faw
another chair	**en stol til**	ehn st**ool** til
ashtray	**et askebeger**	eht **ahs**kehb**ay**gerr
finger bowl	**en skyllebolle**	ehn **shew**llerboller
fork	**en gaffel**	ehn **gahff**erl
glass	**et glass**	eht glahss
knife	**en kniv**	ehn kneev
napkin	**en serviett**	ehn særvy**eht**
pepper-mill	**en pepperkvern**	ehn **pehp**perkv**ǣrn**
plate	**en tallerken**	ehn tahll**ær**kern
serviette	**en serviett**	ehn særvy**eht**
spoon	**en skje**	ehn sh**ay**
toothpick	**en tannpirker**	ehn **tahn**pirkerr

FOR COMPLAINTS, see page 60

EATING OUT

I'd like a/an/some...	Jeg vil gjerne ha...	yay vil yōō'ner haa
aperitif	en aperitiff	ehn ahpehreetif
appetizer	en forrett	ehn forreht
beer	en øl	ehn url
bread	litt brød	lit brūr
butter	litt smør	lit smurr
cabbage	litt kål	lit kawl
cheese	litt ost	lit oost
chips	pommes-frites	pomfrit
coffee	kaffe	kahffer
cole slaw	en hvitkålsalat	ehn veetkawlssahlaat
dessert	en dessert	ehn dehssǣr
fish	fisk	fisk
french fries	pommes-frites	pomfrit
fruit	litt frukt	lit frewkt
game	vilt	vilt
ice-cream	en iskrem	ehn eesskrāym
ketchup	litt ketchup	lit kehtshewp
lemon	litt sitron	lit sitrōōn
lettuce	litt salat	lit sahlaat
meat	kjøtt	khurt
milk	melk	mehlk
mineral water	mineralvann	minnerraalvahn
mustard	litt sennep	lit sehnnerp
noodles	nudler	newdlerr
oil	olje	olyer
pepper	pepper	pehpperr
potatoes	poteter	pootāyterr
poultry	fjærkre	fyǣrkreh
rice	litt ris	lit reess
rolls	noen rundstykker	nōōern rewnsstewkkerr
saccharine	sakkarin	sahkahreen
salad	salat	sahlaat
salt	litt salt	lit sahlt
sandwich	et smørbrød	eht smurrbrūr
seafood	fisk og skalldyr	fisk o skahldewr
seasoning	krydder	krewdderr
soup	en suppe	ehn sewpper
starter	en forrett	ehn forreht
sugar	litt sukker	lit sookkerr
tea	te	teh
vegetables	litt grønnsaker	lit grurnsaakerr
vinegar	litt eddik	lit ehddik
(iced) water	litt (is)vann	lit (eess)vahn
wine	vin	veen

What's on the menu?

Our menu is presented according to courses. Under the headings below you'll find alphabetical lists of dishes that might be offered on a Norwegian menu, with their English equivalents. You can also show the book to the waiter. If you want some fruit, for instance, show him the appropriate list and let him point to what's available. Use pages 41 and 42 for ordering in general.

Here, then, is our guide to good eating and drinking. Turn to the section you want.

	Page
Appetizers	44
Open-face sandwiches—Salads	45
Eggs and omelets	46
Koldtbord	46
Soups	47
Fish and seafood	49
Meat	51
Game and fowl	53
Vegetables	54
Cheese	56
Fruit	57
Dessert	58
Drinks	61
Eating light—Snacks	64

EATING OUT

Obviously, you aren't going to go through every course. If you've had enough say:

| Nothing more, thanks. | **Ikke mer, takk.** | ikker maȳr tahk |

As many dishes are prepared to order, allow time for a main meal. The waiters don't expect you to rush.

Appetizers

It's by no means universal in Norway to take an appetizer before your main course. The Norwegians themselves are usually content with a main—albeit copious—dish, though for a special occasion or a ravenous appetite tasty starters are available in profusion.

In addition to the items listed individually below, many restaurants offer a wide selection of salads and open-face sandwiches (see page 45).

I'd like an appetizer.	**Jeg vil gjerne ha en forrett.**	yay vil yōō'ner haa ehn **forreht**
What do you recommend?	**Hva vil De anbefale?**	vah vil dee **ahn**berfaaler

agurk	ah**gewrk**	cucumber
ansjos	ahn**shōōss**	anchovies
artisjokker	ah'**tishok**kerr	artichokes
assorterte forretter	ahssort**āyr**ter **forreht**terr	hors d'œuvre
blåskjell	**blaw**shehl	mussels
egg	ehg	egg
hårdkokt egg	**hawr**kookt ehg	hard-boiled egg
fruktjuice	**frewkt**yēwss	fruit juice
ananas	ah**nah**nahss	pineapple
appelsin	ahpehl**sseen**	orange
grapefrukt	**grāyp**frewkt	grapefruit
tomat	toom**maat**	tomato
hummer	**hoom**merr	lobster
kaviar	kahvee**aar**	caviar
kaldt kjøtt	kahlt khurt	cold meat
laks	lahks	salmon
røkt	**rūr**kt	smoked
gravet	**graa**vert	cured in salt, sugar and dill
makrell	mah**krehl**	mackerel
marinert	mahrin**āy't**	soused
melon	meh**lōōn**	melon
oliven	oo**lee**vern	olives
fylte	**fewl**ter	stuffed
paprika	**paa**prikah	peppers
reddiker	**rehd**dikerr	radishes
reker	**rāy**kerr	shrimps
salami	sah**laa**mi	salami

sardiner	sah'**dee**nerr	sardines
skinke	**shin**ker	ham
snegler	**snay**lerr	snails
sopp	sop	mushrooms
tunfisk	**tewn**fisk	tunny (tuna)
østers	**urss**tersh	oysters

Open-face sandwiches—Salads

Curious though it may seem to the uninitiated to find a "salad sandwich", there is a supremely practical reason for their close association. The Norwegians are imaginative salad-makers—but more often than not their preparations are served up on slices of bread! This open-face sandwich is called a *smørbrød* (**smurr**brūr), which means, literally, bread and butter.

You may try one as an appetizer, or take two or three as a complete lunch.

The preparations described below are the open-face salad sandwiches you'll encounter most often, though there are many more.

I'd like an sandwich with...	**Jeg vil gjerne ha et smørbrød med...**	yay vil y**æ**'ner haa eht **smurr**brūr m**āy**
italiensk salat (itahli**āy**nsk sah**laat**)	ham, apple, boiled potato, carrots, peas or asparagus and onion or pickles in a mayonnaise dressing	
krabbesalat (**krahb**berssahlaat)	crab meat, celery, lettuce and dill in a mustard dressing	
rekesalat (**rāy**kerssahlaat)	shrimp, apple and celery, sometimes mixed with a tomato dressing, sometimes with a mayonnaise dressing	
russisk salat (**rewss**isk sah**laat**)	carrots, peas, apples, cucumber or gherkins, lettuce and tomatoes in a mayonnaise dressing	
sildesalat (**sill**erssahlaat)	pickled herring, potatoes, beetroot, gherkins, apples and onions mixed together with cream	

If it's a more "conventional" salad you're after, ask:

What salads do you have?	**Hva slags salater har De?**	vah slahkss sah**laa**terr haar dee
agurksalat (ah**gewrk**ssahlaat)	cucumber or gherkins and chopped parsley in a vinegar dressing	
kyllingsalat (**kewl**lingssahlaat)	chicken meat, lettuce, peas, olives and bacon in a vinegar dressing	
vestkystsalat (**vehsst**khewssts- sahlaat)	lobster meat, shrimp, mussels, mushrooms, lettuce, tomatoes and dill in a vinegar dressing	

Eggs

The Norwegians are very fond of eggs, particularly scramb led eggs which they consume with great enthusiasm as an accompaniment to, particularly, ham and cold cuts.

Omelets, while not offered in great variety, include the rather unusual *fruktomelett* (**frewkt**oomerleht), made with fruit and served as a dessert.

bacon og egg	**bay**kern o ehg	bacon and eggs
egg	ehg	egg
eggerøre	**ehg**gerrürrer	scrambled eggs
forlorent egg	fo'**lōō**rernt ehg	poached egg
kokt egg	kookt ehg	boiled egg
en omelett	ehn oomer**leht**	omelet
med sjampinjong	mā̄y shahmpin**yong**	with mushrooms
med skinke	mā̄y **shin**ker	with ham
stekte egg	**stehk**ter ehg	fried eggs

Koldtbord

In Sweden it's called *smörgåsbord*, and it's under that name that this delightful Scandinavian institution is best known throughout the world. The same type of cold buffet is known as *koldtbord* (**kolt**bōōr) in Norway.

In olden days this enormous buffet was a common sight in homes and restaurants. Now the domestic variety has been whittled down and you'll come across it mainly in the larger restaurants, but also in mountain hotels. Though traditionally associated with Christmas, you can now find these beautifully decorated tables brimming with dozens of appetizing delights throughout the year. The big hotels often set up a *koldtbord* on Sundays.

You start at one end of the table, with herring, seafood, salads and other titbits, and return as many times as you like. The price is the same however much you eat.

In addition to fish and seafood there's certain to be a good selection of cold cuts, dried meat and ham. Sometimes you cut your own slices fresh off the joint.

Despite its name, a *koldtbord* always includes a few hot items—meat balls, pork sausages, soup, fried potatoes etc. Scrambled eggs are a favourite, too.

Norwegian country flatbread (*flatbrød*—**flaht**brūr) is often provided. This flat, unleavened cake or cracker made of half barley, half wheat is reminiscent of the Scottish bannock.

Aqua vitae (see page 62) and beer go especially well with all this (it's rare to drink wine with *koldtbord*).

Normally this is a lunchtime experience—which can last up to three hours.

EATING OUT

Soups

I'd like some soup.	**Jeg vil gjerne ha en suppe.**	yay vil yæ'ner haa ehn sewpper
What do you recommend?	**Hva vil De anbefale?**	vah vil dee ahnberfaaler

Soup is often an integral part of a Norwegian meal, whether you eat standing up or sitting down. It's found on a *koldtbord*, too.

Here's a selection of the most common types of soup you're likely to find on the menu:

asparagessuppe	ah**spahr**ggersssewpper	asparagus soup
blomkålsuppe	**blom**kawlssewpper	cauliflower soup
broccolisuppe	**brok**koleessewpper	broccoli soup
gul ertesuppe	gewl **ǣ**'terssewpper	yellow pea soup
grønnsaksuppe	**grurns**sahkssewpper	vegetable soup
hønsesuppe	**hurns**serssewpper	chicken or hen soup
kjøttsuppe	**khurts**sewpper	meat soup or bouillon
krepsesuppe	**krehps**ersssewpper	crawfish soup
kyllingsuppe	**kewll**ingssewpper	chicken soup
løksuppe	**lūrks**sewpper	onion soup
norsk fiskesuppe	noshk **fisk**ersssewpper	Norwegian fish soup
oksehalesuppe	**ookss**erhaalersssewpper	oxtail soup
rekesuppe	**rāy**kersssewpper	shrimp soup
sjampinjongsuppe	shahmpin**yongs**sewpper	mushroom soup
spinatsuppe	spinn**naat**ssewpper	spinach soup
tomatsuppe	toom**maat**ssewpper	tomato soup

While on the subject of soups, there are two which deserve mention almost more as main dishes. They are, in fact, country stews.

One, called *betasuppe* (**bāy**tahssewpper), consists of meat, vegetables and marrow bones. The other, *lapskaus* (**lahps**-kowss), contains chopped pork, diced potatoes, slices of carrots, onions and leeks.

Both of these stews are traditionally eaten with *flatbrød* (**flaht**-brūr), a flat, unleavened cake or cracker, typical of northern Norway.

Fish and seafood

Centuries before Columbus, Leif Erikson and his courageous shipmates made it to "Vinland" thanks to an almost exclusive diet of Atlantic fish caught en route (they did take along supplies of dried, smoked mutton, too).

The traditional Viking fare of fish (mainly herring) and mutton continues to sustain modern Norwegians to a great extent. In the old days fish was simply boiled and served with potatoes and melted butter. More attention was paid to its solid nutritional value than to devising subtle pleasures for the palate. Nowadays, however, the visitor to Norway can regale himself with a much wider choice of fish and seafood prepared in many ways, served with rice or vegetables.

Lobster, salmon, freshwater trout and sea trout are favourites. Cod and flounder are often kept fresh in tanks while awaiting your order.

On the piers of most seaside towns, including Oslo, you can buy prawns or shrimps direct from the boat.

| I'd like some fish. | Jeg vil gjerne ha litt fisk. | yay vil yāö'ner haa lit fisk |
| What kinds of seafood do you have? | Hva slags skalldyr har De? | vah slahkss **skahl**dewr haar dee |

abbor	ahbor	perch
ansjos	ahn**shōōss**	anchovies
blåskjell	blawshehl	mussel
bras	braass	sea bream
gjedde	yehdder	pike
hellefisk	hehllerfisk	halibut
hummer	hoommerr	lobster
hvalkjøtt	vaalkhurt	whale meat
hvitting	vitting	whiting
hyse	**hēw**sser	haddock
karpe	kahrper	carp
kaviar	kahveeaar	caviar
kolje	kolyer	haddock
kreps	krehpss	crayfish
kveite	kvayter	halibut

krabbe	krahbber	crab
laks	lahks	salmon
lutefisk	lewterfisk	codfish steeped in lye
lysing	lewssing	hake
makrell	mahkrehl	mackerel
piggvar	pigvahr	turbot
reker	raykerr	shrimps
rødspette	rurdspehtter	plaice
sardiner	sah'deenerr	sardines
scampi	skahmpi	scampi
sei	say	coalfish
sild	sil	herring
sjøtunge	shurtewnger	sole
sjø-ørret	shururreht	sea trout
småfisk	smawfisk	whitebait
stør	sturr	sturgeon
torsk	toshk	cod
tunfisk	tewnfisk	tunny (tuna)
ørret	urreht	trout
østers	ursstersh	oysters
ål	awl	eel

Here are some of the ways you may have your fish prepared:

baked	ovnstekt	ovnstehkt
cured	saltet, speket	sahltert, spaykert
fried	stekt	stehkt
grilled	grillet	grillert
marinated	marinert	mahrinay't
poached	forloren	fo'loorern
sautéed	brunet i smør	brewnert ee smurr
smoked	røkt	rurkt
steamed	dampet	dahmpert

If you can't decide between fish or meat, you can always compromise by ordering a whale steak (*hvalbiff*—**vaal**bif). It's served with fried onions, boiled potatoes and cranberry jelly.

Meat

As mentioned previously, the Norwegians have a long-standing preference for mutton. But all types of meat are served in restaurants and beef has gained a lot in popularity over recent years, as testified by the proliferation of *steak houses* in the major cities.

The list below will help you decipher the unfamiliar terms on your restaurant menu.

On the following page are descriptions of some specialities you can expect to encounter.

I'd like some...	Jeg vil gjerne ha...	yay vil yææ'ner haa
beef	oksekjøtt	ookserkhurt
mutton	fårekjøtt	fawrerkhurt
pork	svinekjøtt	sveenerkhurt
veal	kalvekjøtt	kahlverkhurt
fenalår	fāynahlawr	cured leg of mutton
fårekotelett	fawrerkotterleht	mutton chop
fårelår	fawrerlawr	leg of mutton
hjerte	yææ'ter	heart
kalv	kahlv	veal
kalvebrissel	kahlverbrisserl	sweetbreads
kalvekjøtt	kahlverkhurt	veal
kalvekotelett	kahlverkotterleht	veal chop
kalvenyrestek	kahlvernēwrersstāyk	loin of veal
kjøttboller	khurtbollerr	meatballs
kjøttkaker	khurtkaakerr	meatburger
kjøttpudding	khurtpewdding	meatloaf
lammekjøtt	lahmmerkhurt	lamb
lever	lehverr	liver
nyrer	nēwrerr	kidneys
oksekjøtt	ookserkhurt	beef
pølser	purlsserr	sausages
ribbe	ribber	spare-ribs
skinke	shinker	ham
smågris	smawgreess	sucking-pig
spekemat	spāykermaat	different sorts of cured meats
stek	stāyk	steak
svinekjøtt	sveenerkhurt	pork
svinelabber	sveenerlabberr	pig's trotters
tunge	toonger	tongue

EATING OUT

Some meat specialities

fenalår
(fāynahlawr)
considered quite a delicacy. It's cured leg of mutton

fårikål
(fawrikawl)
another typical Norwegian dish. It consists of mutton, black pepper and cabbage, all boiled together in a pan

kjøttkaker med surkål
(khurtkaakerr māy sēwrkawl)
meatburgers with sweet-and-sour cabbage; probably the most popular national dish

spekemat
(spāykermaat)
a typical Norwegian dish that comprises a variety of sausages of all colours ranging from red to black, salted and smoked. *Fenalår* (see above) and ham are often included, too. It's eaten with *flatbrød* (see page 47)

spekeskinke
(spāykershinker)
smoked, salted ham—another delight served with thick sour cream and boiled potatoes or with scrambled eggs

All the above dishes are best washed down with aqua vitae *(dram)* and beer.

How do you like your meat?

baked	ovnstekt	ovnstehkt
baked in parchment	ovnstekt i folie	ovnstehkt ee fōōleeer
boiled	kokt	kookt
braised	grytestekt	grēwterstehkt
fried	stekt	stehkt
grilled	grillet	grillert
roasted	ovnstekt	ovnstehkt
sautéed	brunet i smør	brēwnert ee smurr
stewed	stuet	stēwert
underdone (rare)	rå (blodig)	raw (blōōdi)
medium	medium	māydeeewm
well-done	godt stekt	got stehkt

EATING OUT

Game and fowl

Although some larger restaurants feature game on their menus throughout the year, the real season for it is autumn, when it's available in smaller establishments too.

I'd like some game.	**Jeg vil gjerne ha en viltrett.**	yay vil y**ææ'**ner haa ehn **vil**treht
and	ahn'	duck
elg	ehlg	elk
fasan	fah**ssaan**	pheasant
gås	gawss	goose
hare	**haa**rer	hare
hareragu	**haa**rerrahg**gew**	jugged hare
kalkun	kahl**kewn**	turkey
kanin	kah**neen**	rabbit
kylling	**kewl**ling	chicken
kyllinglever	**kewl**linglehverr	chicken livers
bryst	brewst	breast
lår	lawr	leg
vinge	**ving**er	wing
rapphøne	rahp**hūr**ner	partridge
reinsdyr	**rayns**sdewr	reindeer
rugde	**rewg**der	woodcock
rype	**rew**per	ptarmigan
rådyr	**raw**dewr	venison

Some game dishes

elgstek
(**ehlg**ss**tā**yk)
elk—also on the menu in the north

reinsdyrstek
(**rayns**s**dewr**ss**tā**yk)
reindeer—you might find it on the menu in the north of Norway

rype i fløtesaus
(**rew**per ee **flū**rterssowss)
a speciality to look out for; this is a typical Norwegian dish of ptarmigan in a cream sauce

rådyrstek
(**raw**dewrss**tā**yk
another seasonal delicacy is venison

Most game dishes are garnished with a tasty brown sauce and accompanied by potatoes and cranberry (*tyttebær*—**tewt**ter-b**ǣ**r) jam.

Vegetables

Despite Norway's relatively mild winter climate, the growing season for a wide range of vegetables is nevertheless quite short.

Consequently, for the major part of the year the vegetables on a Norwegian's plate are either canned, deep-frozen or imported from southern Europe or even further afield.

All of which goes to explain the national euphoria which greets the appearance in the markets of home-grown produce in summer. That's the time to fill up your plate with delicious beans, carrots or, especially, new potatoes.

What vegetables do you recommend?	Hvilke grønnsaker vil De anbefale?	vilker grurnssahkerr vil dee ahnberfaaler
I prefer some salad.	Jeg foretrekker salat.	yay fawrertrehkkerr sahlaat
agurk	ahgewrk	cucumber
artisjokker	ahrtishokkerr	artichokes
asparges (topper)	ahspahrggerss (topperr)	asparagus (tips)
aspargesbønner	ahspahrggerssburnnerr	haricot beans
blomkål	blomkawl	cauliflower
bønner	burnnerr	beans
erter	æ'terr	peas
gresskar	grehsskaar	marrow
gulrøtter	gewlrurtterr	carrots
hodesalat	hooderssahlaat	lettuce
hvitløk	veetlurk	garlic
kål	kawl	cabbage
linser	linsserr	lentils
mais	maaiss	sweet corn
maiskolbe	maaisskolber	corn on the cob
nepe	nayper	turnips
paprika	paaprikah	peppers
persille	pehrssiller	parsley
poteter	pootayterr	potatoes
purre	pewrrer	leeks
ris	reess	rice
rosenkål	roossernkawl	Brussels sprouts
rødbete	rurbayter	beetroot
rødkål	rurkawl	red cabbage
selleri	sehllerree	celery

EATING OUT

sikori	seekooree	chicory (U.S. endive)
sopp	sop	mushrooms
spinat	spinnaat	spinach
tomater	toomaaterr	tomatoes
trøfler	trurflerr	truffles

Sauces

The most common sauces found in Norway are the three given below.

In addition, a number of renowned sauces of French origin have found their way into the local cuisine—especially béarnaise, hollandaise and béchamel.

brun saus (brewn sowss)	brown sauce; sometimes made with wine, sherry or madeira, and served with meat or fowl
lys saus (lewss sowss)	general description for any light sauce —white wine sauce, curry sauce or horseradish sauce
hvit saus (veet sowss)	white sauce made of milk, mostly served with fish dishes; variations are spiced —with onions, mustard or cheese; also used in soufflés

Salad dressings

If you order a salad, you'll probably have the choice of the following dressings.

eddik-dressing (ehdik-drehssing)	salad dressing of vinegar, oil, salt and pepper
majones-dressing (mahyoonāyss-drehssing)	mayonnaise dressing mixed with cream or thick sour cream and often chives
sennep-dressing (sehnnerp-drehssing)	mustard dressing: mustard, vinegar, oil, salt and pepper

EATING OUT

Cheese

More than 60 varieties of cheese are produced in Norway. Some are imitations of well-known continental brands, using the same cultures. You'll find Norwegian *brie, tilsiter, camembert* and *roquefort* (made with cow's milk it's called *normanna*). Others, like *ridderost* and *jarlsberg*, are indigenous Norwegian cheeses.

But the most typical Norwegian cheeses are *gammelost* (old cheese) and varieties of *brunoster* (brown cheeses). Traditionally, the *gammelost* matured in the straw mattresses of the dairymaids' beds. Alas, this romantic method of production has long ceased and the cheese is now produced in sterile labs. However, the cheese has retained most of its bite.

The *brunoster* aren't strictly speaking cheeses at all, since neither fungi nor curd are used. Instead, the milk (it can be cow's or goat's or a combination of the two, with cream added, or skimmed, or whey) is boiled until practically all the liquid has evaporated.

Cheese specialities

I'd like some cheese.	**Jeg vil gjerne ha litt ost.**	yay vil y**ӕ**'ner haa lit oost

Some Norwegian originals:

blandet geitost, (blahnert **yayt**oost)	mixed cow's and goat's milk, with cream added; the goat's milk flavour is more subtle
gammelost (gahmmerloost)	this typical Norwegian cheese, light yellow-brown in colour, is made of skim-milk; try not to be put off by its strong aroma
nøkkelost (nurkerloost)	spiced with cloves and caraway, this Norwegian cheese originated in Holland
pultost (pewltoost)	sharp, white, caraway-spiced cheese with a rather soft consistency; made of skim-milk

"Brown cheeses"

ekte geitost (**ehk**ter **yayt**oost)	real goat cheese, sometimes with cream added
fløtemysost (**flūr**termewssoost)	made from the whey of cow's milk with cream added; the mildest taste of the lot
Gudbrandsdalsost (**gewd**brahnss-daalssoost)	mild, light-brown cheese made of the whey from cow's and goat's milk
mysost (**mēws**soost)	same as *fløtemysost*, but minus the cream; lean and drier tasting

You may also come across a home-made goat cheese from the mountains, called *stølstype* (**stūr**lsst**ēw**per), and a white variety, similar to the goat cheese of the Balkans.

Fruit

Do you have fresh fruit?	**Har De frisk frukt?**	haar dee frisk frewkt
I'd like a (fresh) fruit salad.	**Jeg vil gjerne ha (frisk) fruktsalat.**	yay vil yǣ'ner haa (frisk) frewktssahlaat
ananas	ahnahnahss	pineapple
appelsin	ahperl**sseen**	orange
aprikos	ahprik**ōōss**	apricot
banan	bahnaan	banana
blåbær	blawbǣr	blueberries
bjørnebær	byur'nerbǣr	blackberries
bringebær	bringerbǣr	raspberries
dadler	dahdlerr	dates
druer	drēwerr	grapes
eple	ehpler	apple
fersken	fæshkern	peach
fikener	feekernerr	figs
grapefrukt	grāypfrewkt	grapefruit
jordbær	yōōrbǣr	strawberries

kastanjer	kahstahnyerr	chestnuts
kirsebær	kheesherbǣr	cherries
kokosnøtt	kookoosnurt	coconut
korinter	koorinterr	currants
mandarin	mahndahreen	tangerine
mandler	mahndlerr	almonds
melon	mehlōōn	melon
multer	mewlterr	cloudberries
nøtter	nurtterr	nuts
plommer	ploommerr	plums
pærer	pǣrerr	pears
rabarbra	rahbahrbrah	rhubarb
rips	rips	red currants
rosiner	roosseenerr	raisins
sitron	sitrōōn	lemon
solbær	sōōlbǣr	black currants
stikkelsbær	stikkerlssbǣr	gooseberries
sviker	svisskerr	prunes
tyttebær	tewtterbǣr	cranberries
valnøtter	vaalnurtterr	walnuts
vannmelon	vahnmehlōōn	watermelon

Dessert

If you've survived all the courses on the menu, you may want to say:

I'd like a dessert, please.	**Jeg vil gjerne ha dessert.**	yay vil yǣ'rner haa dehssǣr
Something light, please.	**Noe lett, er De snill.**	nōōer leht ǣr dee snil
Just a small portion.	**Bare en liten porsjon.**	baarer ehn leetern pooshōōn
Nothing more, thanks.	**Ikke mer, takk.**	ikker māyr tahk

If you are not sure...

What do you have for dessert?	**Hva har De til dessert?**	vah haar dee til dehssǣr

fruktkompott	frewktkoompot	stewed fruit
iskrem	eesskrāym	ice-cream
jordbær	yōōrbǣr	strawberry
mokka	mokkah	coffee
sjokolade	shookoolaader	chocolate
vanilje	vahneelyer	vanilla
karamellpudding	kahrahmehlpewdding	caramel cream
pannekake	pahnnerkaaker	pancake
riskrem	reesskrāym	rice cream

For a typically Norwegian dessert, ask for *multer med krem* (**mewl**terr māy krāym)—cloudberries and whipped cream.

The bill

I'd like to pay.	Jeg vil gjerne betale.	yay vil yǣˈner bertaaler
We'd like to pay separately.	Vi vil gjerne betale hver for oss.	vee vil yǣˈner bertaaler vǣr for oss
You've made a mistake in this bill, I think.	Jeg tror De har gjort en feil på regningen.	yay trōor dee haar yooˈt ehn fayl paw rayningern
What is this amount for?	Hva dekker dette beløpet?	vah dehkkerr dehtter berlūˈrper
Is service included?	Er service inkludert?	ǣr sehrviss inklewdāyˈt
Is everything included?	Er alt inkludert?	ǣr ahlt inklewdāyˈt
Do you accept traveller's cheques?	Tar De reisesjekker?	taar dee rayssershehkkerr
Thank you, this is for you.	Tusen takk, dette er til Dem.	tēwssern tahk, dehtter ǣr til dehm
Keep the change.	Behold resten.	berhol rehsstern

SERVICE INKLUDERT
SERVICE INCLUDED

60

English	Norwegian	Pronunciation
That was a very good meal.	Det var et ut-merket måltid.	dāy vaar eht **ēwt**mǣrkert mawlteed
We enjoyed it, thank you.	Vi nøt det, tusen takk.	vee nūrt dāy **tēw**ssern tahk

Complaints

But perhaps you'll have something to complain about:

English	Norwegian	Pronunciation
That's not what I ordered. I asked for...	Det er ikke det jeg bestilte. Jeg ba om...	dāy ǣr ikker dāy yay berstilter. yay baa om
May I change this?	Kan jeg få byttet dette?	kahn yay faw **bewt**tert **deht**ter
The meat is...	Kjøttet er...	**khurt**ter ǣr
overdone	for mye stekt	for **mēw**er stehkt
underdone (too rare)	for lite stekt	for **lee**ter stehkt
too tough	for seigt	for sayt
This is too...	Det er for...	dāy ǣr for
bitter	bittert	**bitter**'t
salty	salt	sahlt
sweet	søtt	surt
The food is cold.	Maten er kald.	**maa**tern ǣr kahl
This isn't fresh.	Det er ikke ferskt.	dāy ǣr **ik**ker fehshkt
What's taking you so long?	Hvorfor tar det så lang tid?	**voor**for taar dāy saw lahng teed
Where are our drinks?	Hvor er drikke-varene våre?	voor ǣr **drikker**-vahrerner **vaw**rer
This isn't clean.	Denne er ikke ren.	**dehn**ner ǣr ikker rāyn
Would you ask the head waiter to come over?	Vil De be hovmes-teren om å komme hit?	vil dee bāy **hawv**mehss-terrern om aw **kom**mer heet

EATING OUT

Drinks

In common with all the Scandinavian countries, Norway has strict regulations governing the purchase and consumption of alcoholic beverages, especially spirits.

Throughout the country bottled wines and spirits can be bought only in the shops of the State Wine Monopoly (*vinmonopolet*—**veen**moonoopōoler). These stores are found in towns with more than 4,000 inhabitants. Moreover, several small towns entitled to a store have opted for total prohibition (which means that hotels and restaurants there don't serve alcoholic drinks either). Therefore, if you look forward to a nightcap, you'd better keep a supply in reserve.

But "dry" towns are in the minority. At most larger hotels and restaurants, out in the country as well as in the towns, you can order any cocktail or aperitif you like. Spirits, however, are only available during restricted hours—from 3 to 11 p.m., and never on Sunday.

Despite such obstacles Norwegians never appear handicapped in the pursuit of their drinking pleasure.

If you travel to Norway by boat you'll notice that the duty-free bars on board do a lively trade. In contrast to the high prices of alcohol in Norway, the boat (or duty-free airport departure) prices are really attractive. Don't forget to buy your quota. Even if you're a non-drinker, the bottle will make a highly appreciated gift.

EATING OUT

Aperitifs

There is no particularly Norwegian aperitif. For a glass before your meal you'll find internationally known drinks available in the larger hotels and restaurants. If you drink Scotch, you'll probably see your favourite brand on the shelf, but Bourbon is less common.

Beer

Assuming you haven't stumbled upon one of the "dry" towns, you'll encounter a fair choice of beers. You can order any Norwegian beer with confidence.

The light lager, known locally as *Pils* (pilss), goes well with any meal. A darker beer is known as *Bayer* (**bah**yerr). The stronger version of the light lager is *Export* (**eks**po'rt). A stronger Bayer is called *Bokkøl* (**book**url). And finally, a break for the careful motorist: *Brigg* (brig) beer, which is almost non-alcoholic.

Aqua vitae

Akevitt (ahker**veet**), as this potent brew of distilled potatoes or barley is called here, can truly be labelled the national drink of Norway. It contains about 40 per cent pure alcohol, so should be treated with due respect. It is served ice-cold in small glasses.

Akevitt is the usual accompaniment to *koldtbord* and most meat and fish dishes. It's usually chased down with beer.

Wine

No wine is produced in Norway, but imported wines have gained in popularity recently and are widely available.

> **SKÅL!**
> (skawl)
> CHEERS!

I'd like a...of...	Jeg vil gjerne ha...	yay vil y**ōō**'ner haa
glass	et glass	eht glahss
carafe	en karaffel	ehn kahrahfferl
half bottle	en halv flaske	ehn hahl flahssker
bottle	en flaske	ehn flahssker
I'd like to try a glass of...please.	Jeg vil gjerne prøve et glass...	yay vil y**ōō**'ner pr**ūr**ver eht glahss
I want a bottle of white/red wine.	Jeg vil ha en flaske hvit-/rødvin.	yay vil haa ehn **flahss**ker veet/r**ūr**-veen
Do you have open wine?	Har De åpen vin?	haar dee **aw**pern veen

If you enjoyed the wine, you may want to say:

Please bring me another...	Vennligst hent en ...til.	**vehn**ligst hehnt ehn ...til

red	rød	r**ūr**
white	hvit	veet
rosé	rosé	roos**āy**
very dry	meget tørr	m**āy**gert turr
dry	tørr	turr
sweet	søt	s**ūr**t
light	lett	leht
full-bodied	fyldig	fewldi
sparkling	sprudlende	sprewdlehnder
chilled	avkjølt	aavkh**ūr**lt
at room temperature	temperert	tehmperr**āy**'t

Some other alcoholic drinks:

aperitif	aperitiff	ahpehreetif
beer	øl	**ūr**l
cider	eplesider	ehplerseederr
cordial	likør	lik**ūr**r
liqueur	likør	lik**ūr**r
port	portvin	poo'tveen
whisky	whisky	"whisky"
neat (straight)	bar	baar
on the rocks	med isbiter	m**āy** **ee**ssbeeterr

EATING OUT

Other beverages

(hot) chocolate	(varm) sjokolade	(vahrm) shookoolaader
coffee	kaffe	kahffer
cup of coffee	kopp kaffe	kop kahffer
coffee with cream	kaffe med fløte	kahffer may flurter
espresso coffee	expresso-kaffe	ehksprehssookahffer
fruit juice	fruksaft	frewktssahft
apple	eple	ehpler
grapefruit	grapefrukt	grāypfrewkt
lemon	sitron	sitrōon
orange	appelsin	ahperlsseen
pineapple	ananas	ahnahnahss
tomato	tomat	toommaat
lemonade	sitronbrus	sitrōonbrewss
milk	melk	mehlk
milkshake	milkshake	milkshayk
mineral water	mineralvann	minnerraal-vahn
orangeade	brus	brewss
squash (soda pop)	saft	sahft
tea	te	teh
with milk/lemon	med melk/sitron	may mehlk/sitrōon
iced tea	is-te	eess-teh

Eating light—Snacks

I'll have one of those, please.	Jeg vil gjerne ha én av dem.	yay vil yǣᴇrner haa āyn ahv dehm
Please give me a/an some...	Vil De være så snill å gi meg...	vil dee vǣᴇrer saw snil aw yee may
biscuits (Br.)	noen kjeks	nōoern khehks
bread	litt brød	lit brūr
butter	litt smør	lit smurr
cake	en kake	ehn kaaker
candy	litt sukkertøy	lit sookkerrtoy
chocolate bar	en sjokoladeplate	ehn shookoolaaderplaater
cookies	noen kjeks	nōoern khehks
frankfurter	en varm pølse	ehn vahrm purlsser
hamburger	en hamburger	ehn hahmburgerr
hot-dog	en hot dog	ehn hot dog
ice-cream	en iskrem	ehn eesskrāym
pastry	noen konditorkaker	nōoern kondeetoorkaakerr
roll	et rundstykke	eht rewnstewkker
sandwich	et smørbrød	eht smurrbrūr
sweets	litt sukkertøy	lit sookkertoy

Travelling around

Plane

Very brief—because at any airport or airline office you're almost certain to find someone who speaks English.

Do you speak English?	**Snakker De engelsk?**	snahkkerr dee ehngerlsk
Is there a flight to Bergen?	**Går det et fly til Bergen?**	gawr dāy eht flew til bærgern
Is it a nonstop flight?	**Er turen uten mellomlandinger?**	ār tēwrern ēwtern mehllomlahndingerr
When's the next plane to Bodø?	**Når går neste fly til Bodø?**	nawr gawr nehsster flew til boōdur
Do I have to change planes?	**Må jeg bytte fly?**	maw yay bewtter flew
Can I get to Stavanger today?	**Kan jeg komme til Stavanger i dag?**	kahn yay kommer til stahvahngerr ee daag
I'd like a ticket to Trondheim.	**Jeg vil gjerne ha en billett til Trondheim**	yay vil yǣ'ner haa ehn billeht til tronhaym
What's the fare to Bergen?	**Hva koster det til Bergen?**	vah kossterr dāy til bærgern
single (one-way)	**én vei**	āyn vay
return (roundtrip)	**tur-retur**	tewr-rāytēwr
economy	**turistklasse**	tewrist-klahsser
first class	**første klasse**	furshter klahsser
Is there an excursion fare?	**Har De en billigtur?**	haar dee ehn billitēwr
What time does the plane take off?	**Når går flyet?**	nawr gawr flēwer
What time do I have to check in?	**Når må jeg være på flyplassen?**	nawr maw yay vǣrer paw flēwplahssern

ANKOMST	**AVGANG**
ARRIVAL	DEPARTURE

| What's the flight number? | **Hva er flight-nummeret?** | vah **ær flayt**noommerrer |
| What time do we arrive? | **Når er vi fremme?** | nawr **ær** vee **frehm**mer |

Train

Trains in Norway are operated by *Norges Statsbaner* which also has quite an extensive bus network covering a considerable part of the country.

There are various types of trains. A sleeper can be had at a reasonable extra charge. Timetables can be obtained free of charge. Reservations are not normally necessary for short-distance travel but are recommended on long-distance trains, and during the Christmas and Easter periods you should book your seat well ahead.

Types of trains

Utenlandstog (ēwtehnlahnsstawg)	International express, stopping at main stations only
Ekspress (eksprehss)	Long-distance express stopping at main stations only; one class only
Hurtigtog (Ht.) (hewrteetawg)	Long-distance express stopping at main stations only
Lokaltog (Lt.) (lookaaltawg)	Local train stopping at all stations, unless otherwise indicated
Forstadstog (Ft.) (fawshtahdsstawg)	Suburban train
Dagtog (daagtawg)	Long-distance day train
Nattog (nahttawg)	Long-distance night train, composed mainly of sleeping-cars
Sovevogn (sawvervongn)	Sleeper consisting of compartments with two (1st class) and three (2nd class) beds and washing facilities; reservations necessary
Spisevogn (speesservongn)	Dining-car

To the railway station

Where's the railway station?	Hvor er jernbane-stasjonen?	voor ær yǣ'nbaaner-stashōōnern
Taxi, please!	Drosje!	drosher
Take me to the railway station.	Kjør meg til jernbane-stasjonen.	khūrr may til yǣ'n-baanerstashōōnern
What's the fare?	Hvor mye blir det?	voor mēwer bleer dāy

Where's the...?

Where's the...?	Hvor er...?	voor ær
bar	baren	baarern
barber's shop	frisørsalongen	frissūrrsahlongern
buffet	buffeten	bewffāyern
currency exchange office	vekslingskontoret	vehkslingsskoontōōrer
information office	informasjonskontoret	informashōōnskoontōōrer
left luggage office	reisegodsopp-bevaringen	rayssergoodssop-bervaaringern
lost property (lost and found) office	hittegodskontoret	hittehgoodsskoontōōrer
luggage lockers	oppbevaringsboksene	opbervaaringssbokserner
newsstand/bookstall	aviskiosken/bok-kiosken	ahveesskhioskern/bōōk-khioskern
platform 7	plattform 7	plahtform 7
reservation office	reservasjonsluken	rāysærvahshōōnsslewkkern
restaurant	restauranten	rehsterrahngern
ticket office	billettluken	billehttlewkkern
toilets	toalettet	tooahlehtter
waiting room	venterommet	vehnterroommer
Where are the toilets?	Hvor er toalettet?	voor ær tooahlehtter

INNGANG	ENTRANCE
UTGANG	EXIT
TIL PLATTFORMENE	TO THE PLATFORMS

FOR TAXI, see page 27

TRAVELING AROUND

Inquiries

Note: In Norway i means information office.

When is the...train to Bergen?	Når går...tog til Bergen?	nawr gawr... tawg til **bæær**gern
first	**første**	**fursh**ter
last	**siste**	**siss**ter
next	**neste**	**nehss**ter
What time does the train for Trondheim leave?	Når går toget til Trondheim?	nawr gawr **tawg**ger til **tron**haym
What's the fare to Stavanger?	Hva koster det til Stavanger?	vah **koss**terr dāy til stah**vahng**err
Is it a through train?	Er det et direkte tog?	āēr dāy eht di**rehk**ter tawg
Will the train leave on time?	Kommer toget til å gå presist?	**kom**mer **tawg**ger til aw gaw preh**ss**seesst
Is the train late?	Er toget forsinket?	āēr **tawg**ger fo**shing**kert
What time does the train arrive at Stavanger?	Når skal toget være fremme i Stavanger?	nawr skahl **tawg**ger **vāē**rer **frehm**mer ee stah**vahng**err
Is there a dining-car on the train?	Er det spisevogn på toget?	āēr dāy **spees**servongn paw **tawg**ger
Is there a sleeping-car on the train?	Er det sovevogn på toget?	āēr dāy **saw**vervongn paw **tawg**ger
Does the train stop at Lillehammer?	Stopper toget i Lillehammer?	**stop**per **tawg**ger ee **lille**rhahmmerr
What platform does the train for Kongsberg leave from?	Fra hvilken plattform går toget til Kongsberg?	frah vilkern **plaht**form gawr **tawg**ger til **kongss**bærg
What platform does the train from Oslo arrive at?	I hvilket spor kommer toget fra Oslo?	ee **vil**kert spoor **kom**mer **tawg**ger fra **ooss**loo

---

TURISTINFORMASJON	TOURIST INFORMATION
VEKSLINGSKONTOR	CURRENCY EXCHANGE

Det er et direkte tog.	It's a through train.
De må bytte i...	You have to change at...
Plattform...er...	Platform...is...
der borte	over there
opp trappen	upstairs
til venstre	on the left
til høyre	on the right
Det går et tog til... klokken...	There's a train to... at...
Toget Deres vil gå fra plattform / spor...	Your train will leave from platform...
Det blir en forsinkelse på...minutter.	There'll be a delay of... minutes.

TRAVELLING AROUND

Tickets

I want a ticket to Oslo.	Jeg vil ha en billett til Oslo.	yay vil haa ehn billeht til oossloo
single (one-way)	én vei	āyn vay
return (roundtrip)	tur-retur	tewr-rāytewr
first class	første klasse	furshter klahsser
second class	annen klasse	ahnnern klahsser
Must the boy/girl pay the full fare?	Må gutten/piken betale full pris?	maw gewttern/peekern bertaaler fewl preess
He's/She's 13.*	Han er/Hun er 13.	hahn ær/hewn ær 13
I'd like to reserve a seat.	Jeg vil gjerne bestille en plass.	yay vil yǣ'ner berstiller ehn plahss

Første eller annen klasse?	First or second class?
Røykere/Ikke-røykere?	Smoker/Non smoker?
Vindusplass?	Window seat?
Hvor gammel er han/hun?	How old is he/she?

* In Norway children up to the age of 4 travel free; those between 4 and 15 pay half fare.

All aboard...

Is this the right platform for the train to Bergen?	Er dette den riktige plattformen for toget til Bergen?	**æ**r **deht**ter dehn **rik**teeer **plaht**formern for **tawg**ger til **bær**gern
Is this the right train to Trondheim?	Er dette toget til Trondheim?	**æ**r **deht**ter **tawg**ger til **tron**haym
Excuse me. May I get by?	Unnskyld. Kan jeg få komme forbi?	**ewn**shewl. kahn yay faw **kom**mer for**bee**
Is this seat taken?	Er denne plassen opptatt?	**æ**r **dehn**ner **plahss**ern **op**taht

---

RØYKING FORBUDT
NO SMOKING

I think that's my seat.	Jeg tror at dette er min plass.	yay **troo**r aht **deht**ter **æ**r meen plahss
Would you let me know before we get to Drammen?	Vil De gi meg beskjed når vi kommer til Drammen?	vil dee yee may ber**shay** nawr vee **kom**merr til **drahm**mern
What station is this?	Hvilken stasjon er dette?	**vil**kern stah**shoon æ**r **deht**ter
How long does the train stop here?	Hvor lenge står toget her?	voor **lehn**ger stawr **tawg**ger **hæ**r
When do we get to Hamar?	Når kommer vi til Hamar?	nawr **kom**merr vee til **haa**mahr

Sometime on the journey the ticket collector (*billettøren*—billeh**tür**rern) will come around and say: *Kan jeg få se billettene, takk?* (Tickets, please!).

Eating

If you want a full meal in the dining car (*spisevognen*—**spees**servongnern), you have to get a ticket from the attendant who'll come to your compartment. There are usually two sittings for lunch and dinner. State which one you prefer.

| First/Second sitting for dinner. | Første/Annen bordsetning til middag. | furshter/ahnnern bōōrssehtning til middaag |
| Where's the dining car? | Hvor er spisevognen? | voor ær speesservongnern |

Sleeping

Are there any free compartments in the sleeping-car?	Er det noen ledige kupéer i sovevognen?	ær dāy nōōern lāydeeer kewpāyerr ee sawvervongnern
Where's the sleeping-car?	Hvor er sovevognen?	voor ær sawvervongnern
Where's my berth?	Hvor er min køye?	voor ær meen koyer
Compartments 18 and 19, please.	Kupé nr. 18 og 19, er De snill.	kewpāy noommerr 18 o 19 ær dee snil
I'd like an upper/lower berth.	Jeg vil gjerne ha den øverste/nederste køyen.	yay vil yǣ'ner haa dehn ūrverrsster/nāyderrsster koyern
Would you make up our berths?	Vil De gjøre i stand køyene våre?	vil dee yūrrer ee stahn koyerner vawrer
Would you call me at 7 o'clock?	Vil De være vennlig å vekke meg kl. 7?	vil dee vǣrer vehnli aw vehkker may klokkern 7
Would you bring me some coffee in the morning?	Kan jeg få litt kaffe i morgen tidlig?	kahn yay faw lit kahffer ee mawern teeli

Baggage and porters

| Can you help me with my bags? | Kan De hjelpe meg med mine kofferter? | kahn dee yehlper may māy meener kooffeh'terr |
| Please put them down here. | Vær så snill å sette dem her. | vǣr saw snil aw sehter dehm hǣr |

Note: If you wish, you can have your luggage put in the guard's van (baggage car) of your train. There's an extra charge for *reisegods* (**rayss**ergoodss) service. You have to collect your bags at the end of the trip.

FOR PORTERS, see also page 24

TRAVELLING AROUND

Lost!

We hope you'll have no need for the following phrases on your trip...but just in case:

Where's the lost property office (lost and found)?	**Hvor er hittegods-kontoret?**	voor ær hittegooss-koontoorer
I've lost my...	**Jeg har mistet...**	yay haar misstert
this morning yesterday	**i morges** **i går**	ee morrerss ee gawr
I lost it in...	**Jeg mistet det i...**	yay misstert day ee
It's very valuable.	**Det er veldig verdifullt.**	day ær vehldi væ'deefewlt

Timetables

If you intend to do a lot of rail travelling, it might be a good idea to buy a timetable. Ticket and inquiry offices and some bookshops sell compact, country-wide train schedules.

I'd like to buy a timetable.	**Jeg vil gjerne ha en togtabell.**	yay vil yæ'ner haa ehn tawgtahbehl

Underground (subway)

Oslo's equivalent of the London Underground or the New York Subway is the *T-banen* (**tay**baanern), extending from the centre of the capital to the suburbs. A route map is displayed outside every station. News-stands and travel agents have pocket maps. The *T-banen* runs from 5.50 a.m. till 1.30 a.m.

Where's the nearest underground station?	**Hvor er nærmeste T-banestasjon?**	voor ær nærmerhsster tay-baanerstahshoon
Does this train go to...?	**Går dette toget til...?**	gawr dehtter tawgger til
Is the next station...?	**Er neste stasjon...?**	ær nehsster stahshoon

Bus—Tram (streetcar)

Depending on the vehicle, you either pay your fare when you enter, or buy a ticket from the roving conductor. Runabout tickets and booklets of tickets are sold at the bus terminals as well as on the bus or tram itself.

English	Norwegian	Pronunciation
I'd like a booklet of tickets.	Jeg vil gjerne ha et billetthefte.	yay vil yææ'ner haa eht billehtthehfter
I'd like a runabout ticket.	Jeg vil gjerne ha en rundreisebillett.	yay vil yææ'ner haa ehn rewnraysserbilleht
Where can I get a bus to the opera house?	Hvorfra kan jeg ta en buss til operaen?	voorfrah kahn yay taa ehn bewss til ōōperrahern
Where's the bus stop/terminus?	Hvor er bussholdeplassen/terminalen?	voor ær bewssholderplahssern/tærminaalern
When is the...bus to Hønefoss	Når går...buss til Hønefoss?	nawr gawr...bewss til hūrnerfoss
first	første	furshter
last	siste	sisster
next	neste	nehsster
How often do the buses go to Snarøya?	Hvor ofte går bussene til Snarøya?	voor ofter gawr bewsserner til snaaroyah
How much is the fare to...?	Hva koster det til...?	vah kossterr dāy til
Do I have to change buses?	Må jeg bytte buss?	maw yay bewtter bewss
Can I have a transfer ticket?	Kan jeg få en overgangsbillett?	kahn yay faw ehn awverrgahngssbilleht
How long does the journey take?	Hvor lang tid tar turen?	voor lahng teed taar tewrern
Will you tell me when to get off?	Vil De være så snill å si fra når jeg skal gå av?	vil dee væærer saw snil aw see fraa nawr yay skahl gaw ahv

TRAVELLING AROUND

BUSSHOLDEPLASS	REGULAR BUS STOP
STOPPER PÅ SIGNAL	STOPS ON REQUEST

I want to get off at the National Theatre.	Jeg skal av ved Nasjonalteatret.	yay skahl ahv väy nahshōōnaaltäyaatrer
Please let me off at the next stop.	Kan De la meg komme av på neste stoppested.	kahn dee laa may kommer ahv paw nehsster stopperstäyd
May I please have my luggage?	Kan jeg få min bagasje?	kahn yay faw meen bahgaasher

Boat services

Coastal express steamers *(hurtigruta)* operate along the Norwegian coast from Bergen up to North Cape.

Cruise ships travel the fjords, offering spectacular views of this part of Norway from sea-level.

Information on the many tours available may be obtained from any travel agent.

Ferries ship you and your car across Norway's many rivers and fjords. You're bound to come across them on the main coastal roads in the south, west and north of the country.

Other means of transport

bicycle	sykkel	sewkkerl
boat	båt	bawt
houseboat	husbåt	hewssbawt
motorboat	motorbåt	mōōtoorbawt
rowing boat	robåt	rōōbawt
sailing boat	seilbåt	saylbawt
ferry	ferge	færger
helicopter	helikopter	hehlikopterr
hitch-hiking	haiking	hayking
horse-riding	ridning	reedning
hovercraft	luftputefartøy	lewftpewterfaartoy
moped (motor-bike)	moped	moopäyd
motorcycle	motorsykkel	mōōtoorssewkkerl

And if you're really stuck, start...

| walking | å spasere | aw spahssäyrer |

TRAVELLING AROUND

Around and about—Sightseeing

Here we're more concerned with the cultural aspect of life than with entertainment; and, for the moment, with towns rather than the countryside. If you want a guide book, ask...

Can you recommend a good guide book on...?	Kan De anbefale en god guidebok for...?	kahn dee ahnbehfaaler ehn gōō gaydbōōk for
Is there a tourist office here?	Er det et turist-kontor her?	ǣr dāy eht tēwrist-koontōōr hǣr
Where's the tourist office?	Hvor er turist-kontoret?	voor ǣr tēwrist-koontōōrer
What are the main points of interest?	Hva er de mest interessante severdig-hetene?	vah ǣr dee mehsst interr-ehssahnger sāyvǣrdi-hāyterner
We're here for...	Vi skal være her...	vee skahl vǣrer hǣr
only a few hours	bare noen få timer	baarer nōōern faw teemerr
a day	én dag	āyn daag
3 days	3 dager	3 daagerr
a week	en uke	ehn ēwker
Can you recommend a (city) sightseeing tour?	Kan De anbefale en sightseeing-tur (i byen)?	kahn dee ahnbehfaaler ehn saytseeing-tēwr (ee bēwern)
Where does the bus start from?	Hvorfra går bussen?	voorfrah gawr bewssern
Will it pick us up at the hotel?	Henter den oss ved hotellet?	hehnterr dehn oss vāy hootehller
What bus/tram (street-car) should we take?	Hvilken buss/trikk skal vi ta?	vilkern bewss/trik skahl vee taa
How much does the tour cost?	Hvor meget koster turen?	voor māygert kossterr tēwrern
What time does the tour start?	Når starter turen?	nawr stah'terr tēwrern
What time do we get back?	Når kommer vi tilbake?	nawr kommerr vee tilbaaker
We'd like to rent a car for the day.	Vi vil gjerne leie en bil i dag.	vee vil yǣ'ner layer ehn beel ee daag

FOR TIME OF DAY, see page 178

SIGHTSEEING

Is there an English speaking guide?	Finnes det en engelsktalende guide?	finners dāy ehn ehngerlsktaalerndr gayd
Where is/Where are the...?	Hvor er...?	voor ǣr
abbey	klostret	klosstrer
aquarium	akvariet	ahkvaarier
amusement park	fornøyelsesparken	foornoyerlssersspahrkern
art gallery	kunstgalleriet	kewnsst-gahlerreeer
beach	stranden	strahndern
botanical gardens	botanisk hage	bootaanisk haager
bridge	broen	brōōern
building	bygningen	bewgningern
business district	forretningsstrøket	forrehtningsstrūrker
castle	slottet	slotter
cathedral	domkirken	domkheerkern
cemetery	kirkegården	kheerkergawrern
city centre	sentrum (i byen)	sehntrewm (ee bēwern)
city hall	rådhuset	rawdhēwsser
church	kirken	kheerkern
concert hall	konserthuset	koonsseh'thēwsser
convent	klostret	klosstrer
court house	rettssalen	rehtssaalern
docks	dokkene	dokkerner
downtown area	sentrum (i byen)	sehntrewm (ee bēwern)
exhibition	utstillingen	ēwtstillingern
factory	fabrikken	fahbrikkern
fortress	festningen	fehsstningern
fountain	fontenen	fontāynern
gardens	parkene	pahrkerner
harbour	havnen	hahvnern
lake	innsjøen	inshūrern
library	biblioteket	bibliootāyker
market	torget	torger
memorial	minnesmerket	minnehssmehrker
monastery	klostret	klosstrer
monument	monumentet	moonewmehnter
museum	museet	mewssāyer
observatory	observatoriet	obsǣrvahtōōrier
old city	gamlebyen	gahmlerbēwern
opera house	operaen	ōōperrahern
palace	slottet	slotter
park	parken	pahrkern
parliament building	Stortinget	stōōrtinger
river	elven	ehlvern
royal palace	det kongelige slott	dāy kongerleeer slot

FOR ASKING THE WAY, see page 144

seafront	strandpromenaden	strahnproomehnaadern
shopping centre	shopping-senteret	shopping-sehnterrer
shrine	helligdommen	hehllidommern
stadium	stadion	staadyoon
statue	statuen	staatewern
stock exchange	børsen	bŭrshern
swimming pool	svømmebassenget	svurmmerbahssehnger
synagogue	synagogen	sewnahgōōgern
television studios	fjernsynshuset	fyǣ'nssewnsshewsser
theatre	teatret	tāyaatrer
tomb	graven	graavern
tower	tårnet	taw'ner
university	universitetet	ewnivehshitāyter
watermill	vannmøllen	vahnmurllern
zoo	zoologisk hage	sōōlawggisk haager

Admission

Is...open on Sundays?	Er...åpent om søndagene?	ǣr...awpernt om surndaagerner
When does it open/close?	Når åpner/stenger det?	nawr awpnerr/stehngerr dāy
Where do I get tickets?	Hvor får jeg kjøpt billetter?	voor fawr yay khurpt billehtterr
How much is the entrance fee?	Hvor mye koster det å komme inn?	voor mēwer kossterr dāy aw kommer in
Is there any reduction for students/children?	Er det reduksjon for studenter/barn?	ǣr dāy rāydewkshōōn for stewdehnterr/baa'n
Have you a guide book in English?	Har De en guidebok på engelsk?	haar dee ehn gayd-book paw ehngerlsk
Can I buy a catalogue?	Kan jeg få kjøpt en katalog?	kahn yay faw khurpt ehn kahtahlōōg
Is it all right to take pictures?	Er det tillatt å fotografere?	ǣr dāy tillaht aw footoograhfāyrer

SIGHTSEEING

| GRATIS ADGANG | ADMISSION FREE |
| FOTOGRAFERING IKKE TILLATT | NO CAMERAS ALLOWED |

Who—What—When?

What's that building?	**Hvilken bygning er det?**	vilkern **bewgg**ning **ǣr** dāy
Who was the...?	**Hvem var...?**	vehm vaar
architect	**arkitekten**	ahrki**tehk**tern
artist	**kunstneren**	**kewnsst**nehrern
painter	**maleren**	**maa**lehrern
sculptor	**billedhoggeren**	**billeh**dhoggehrern
Who built it?	**Hvem bygde det?**	vehm **bewg**der dāy
Who painted that picture?	**Hvem har malt det bildet?**	vehm haar maalt dāy **bil**lder
When did he live?	**Når levde han?**	nawr **lāy**vder hahn
When was it built?	**Når ble det bygd?**	nawr blāy dāy bewgd
Where's the house where...lived?	**Hvor er huset der ...levde?**	voor **ǣr hew**sser dǣr ...**lāy**vder
We're interested in...	**Vi er interessert i...**	vee **ǣr** interrer**ssāy't** ee
antiques	**antikviteter**	ahntikvi**tāy**terr
archaeology	**arkeologi**	ahrkehoo**loo**ggee
art	**kunst**	kewnsst
botany	**botanikk**	boo**tah**nik
ceramics	**keramikk**	kheh**rah**mik
coins	**mynter**	**mewn**terr
crafts	**håndtverk**	**hawnt**værk
fine arts	**bildende kunst**	**bil**dernde kewnsst
folk art	**folklore kunst**	folk**lōō**rer kewnsst
furniture	**møbler**	**murb**lerr
geology	**geologi**	gehoo**loo**ggee
history	**historie**	his**tōō**reeer
medicine	**medisin**	mehdi**sseen**
music	**musikk**	mew**ssik**
natural history	**naturhistorie**	nah**tewr**hisstōōreeer
ornithology	**ornitologi**	oornitoo**loo**ggee
painting	**kunstmaling**	**kewnsst**maaling
pottery	**pottemakeri**	**pott**ermaakerree
prehistory	**fortidshistorie**	**for**tidshisstōōreeer
sculpture	**billedhoggerkunst**	**bil**lehdhoggerkewnsst
wild life	**dyreliv**	**dew**rerleev
zoology	**zoologi**	soo-oo**loo**ggee
Where's the... department?	**Hvor er avdelingen for...**	voor **ǣr** ahv**dāy**lingern for

Just the adjective you've been looking for...

It's...	Det er...	dāy ǣr
amazing	forbausende	forbowssernder
awful	fryktelig	frewkterli
beautiful	vakkert	vahkker't
delightful	deilig	dayli
disappointing	skuffende	skewffernder
gloomy	mørkt	murrkt
impressive	imponerende	impoonāyrernder
incomparable	uforlignelig	ēwforlingnehli
interesting	interessant	interrerssahnt
mediocre	middelmådig	midderlmawdi
overwhelming	overveldende	awverrvehlddernder
strange	merkelig	mǣhrkehli
superb	herlig	hǣr'li
terrifying	skremmende	skrehmmernder

Religious services

The national religion of Norway is the Evangelical Lutheran Church. Almost 98 per cent of the population belongs to the state church. There is, however, complete freedom of religion. To visit a church, apply to the sexton. Don't be surprised if you're asked a small entrance fee in some of the oldest and most interesting churches. Tourist interest helps to pay for the upkeep.

Is there a/an... near here?	Er det en... i nærheten?	ǣr dāy ehn... ee nǣrhehtern
Catholic church	katolsk kirke	kahtōōlsk kheerker
Protestant church	protestantisk kirke	prooterstahntisk kheerker
synagogue	synagoge	sewnahgōōgger
At what time is...?	Når begynner...?	nawr beryewnnerr
mass	messen	mehssern
the service	gudstjenesten	gewdsstyāynersstern
Where can I find a... who speaks English?	Hvor kan jeg finne en...som snakker engelsk?	voor kahn yay finner ehn...som snahkkerr ehngerlsk
priest/minister/ rabbi	katolsk prest/prest/ rabbiner	kahtōōlsk prehsst/prehsst/ rahbbeenerr

Relaxing

Cinema (movies)—Theatre

Films are shown with the original soundtrack and have subtitles in Norwegian. In several cinemas programmes begin at fixed hours—usually 5, 7 and 9 p.m.—and no one is admitted after the performance has begun.

For stage plays advance booking is advisable. Curtain time is around 8 p.m. Incidentally, the cloakroom charge is included in the ticket price; never tip the usherette.

Newspapers and billboards advertise current attractions.

What's showing at the cinema tonight?	**Hva går på kino i kveld?**	vah gawr paw **khee**noo ee kvehl
What's playing at the...Theatre?	**Hva går på ...teatret?**	vah gawr paw ...tāȳaatrer
What sort of play is it?	**Hva slags stykke er det?**	vah slahkss **stewk**ker ǣr dāȳ
Who's it by?	**Hvem har skrevet det?**	vehm haar **skrāȳ**vert dāȳ
Can you recommend (a)...?	**Kan De anbefale ...?**	kahn dee **ahn**berfaaler
good film	**en god film**	ehn gōō film
comedy	**en komedie**	ehn koo**māȳ**deeer
something light	**noe lett**	**nōō**er leht
drama	**et drama**	eht **draa**mah
musical	**en musical**	ehn **myēw**ssikahl
revue	**en revy**	ehn reh**vēw**
thriller	**en spennende film**	ehn **spehn**nernder film
western	**en western**	ehn **vehss**ter'n
At what theatre is that new play by... being performed?	**På hvilket teater går det nye stykket av...?**	paw **vil**kert tāȳaaterr gawr dāȳ **nēȳ**er **stewk**ker ahv
Where's that new film by...being shown?	**Hvor går den nye filmen av...?**	voor gawr dehn **nēȳ**er **film**ern ahv

Who's in it?	Hvem spiller i den?	vehm **spiller** ee dehn
Who's playing the lead?	Hvem har hoved-rollen?	vehm haar **hōō**verd-rollern
Who's the director?	Hvem er regissør?	vehm **ær** rehshiss**ūrr**
What time does it begin/end?	Når begynner/slutter den?	nawr beh**yewn**nerr/**slewt**terr dehn
What time does the first evening performance start?	Når er første kveldsforestilling?	nawr **ær** **furrsh**ter **kvehlss**fawrersstilling
Are there any tickets for tonight?	Har De noen billetter til i kveld?	haar dee **nōō**ern bill**eht**terr til ee kvehl

---

Dessverre, det er utsolgt.	I'm sorry, we're sold out.
Det er bare noen få plasser igjen i...	There are only a few seats left in the...
parkett	stalls (orchestra)
første losjerad	circle (balcony)
Det er bare ståplasser igjen.	There's standing room only.
Kan jeg få se Deres billett?	May I see your ticket?
Dette er Deres plass.	This is your seat.

RELAXING

How much are the tickets?	Hva koster billettene?	vah **koss**terr bill**eht**terner
I want to reserve 2 tickets for the show on Friday evening.	Jeg vil gjerne be-stille 2 billetter til forestillingen fredag kveld.	yay vil **yær**ner ber-stiller 2 bill**eht**terr til **fawr**ersstillingern **frāy**daag kvehl
May I please have a programme?	Kan jeg få et program?	kahn yay faw eht proo**grahm**
Can I check this coat?	Kan jeg henge fra meg kåpen?	kahn yay **heng**er fraa may **kaw**pern
Can I have a ticket for the matinée on Tuesday?	Kan jeg få en billett til matinéen tirsdag?	kahn yay faw ehn bill**eht** til mahtin**āy**ern **teesh**daag

I'd like a box for 4.	Jeg vil gjerne ha en losje til 4.	yay vil y**ǣ'**ner haa ehn l**ōō**sher til 4
I want a seat in the stalls (orchestra).	Jeg vil gjerne ha en plass i parkett.	yay vil y**ǣ'**ner haa ehn plahss ee pahr**keht**
Not too far back.	Ikke for langt bak.	**ik**ker for lahngt baak
Somewhere in the middle.	Et sted midt på.	eht st**āy** mit paw
How much are the seats in the circle? (balcony)?	Hva koster billettene i første losjerad?	vah **koss**terr bil**leht**terner ee **furshter** l**ōō**sherraad

Opera—Ballet—Concert

Where's the opera house?	Hvor ligger operaen?	voor **liggerr ōō**perrahern
Where's the concert hall?	Hvor ligger konserthuset?	voor **liggerr** kons**seh't**-h**ew**sser
What's on at the opera tonight?	Hva går på operaen i kveld?	vah gawr paw **ōō**perrahern ee kvehl
Who's singing?	Hvem synger?	vehm **sewng**err
Who's dancing?	Hvem danser?	vehm **dahns**serr
What time does the programme start?	Når begynner forestillingen?	nawr be**hyewn**nerr **faw**rersstillingern
What orchestra is playing?	Hvilket orkester spiller?	**vilkert** or**kehss**terr **spiller**
What's on the programme?	Hva står på programmet?	vah stawr paw proo-**grahm**mer
Who's the soloist?	Hvem er solist?	vehm **ǣr** soolist
Who's the conductor?	Hva heter dirigenten?	vah **hāy**terr diri**ggehn**tern

Nightclubs—Taverns

Nightclubs, of course, are a feature of the larger towns only. There you may find quite a lot of places open for dancing from 11 p.m. until 4 a.m.

In the countryside, the night-life is confined to the biggest—or often the only—hotel in a town. This will be the place where people meet, with dancing once or twice a week. If there is no hotel or other likely centre, look for what's called the *lokalet* (loo**kaa**ler)—the village hall.

Sometimes in summer folk music and dancing in national costume (*bunad*—**bew**nahd) is especially arranged for tourists.

Dress: For nightclubs, casual dress raises eyebrows; men should wear a jacket and tie.

Can you recommend a good nightclub/cabaret?	**Kan De anbefale en god nattklubb/kabaret?**	kahn dee **ahn**behfaaler ehn goo **naht**klewb/kahbahr**ay**
Is there a floor show?	**Er det "floor show" der?**	aer day **flawr**show daer
What time does the floor show start?	**Når begynner "floor showet"?**	nawr ber**yew**nerr **flawr**shower
Is a dark suit/evening dress necessary?	**Er det nødvendig med mørk dress/aftenkjole?**	aer day nurd**veh**ndi may murrk drehss/**ahftern**khooler

And once inside...

A table for 2, please.	**Jeg vil gjerne ha et bord til 2.**	yay vil y**ae**'ner haa eht boor til 2
My name's... I've reserved a table for 4.	**Mitt navn er... Jeg har bestilt et bord til 4.**	mit nahvn aer... yay haar ber**stil**t eht boor til 4
I telephoned you earlier.	**Jeg har ringt tidligere.**	yay haar ringt **tee**leeehrer
We haven't got a reservation.	**Vi har ikke bestilt bord.**	vee haar **ik**ker ber**stil**t boor

RELAXING

Dancing

Where can we go dancing?	Hvor kan vi gå å danse?	voor kahn vee gaw aw **dahnsser**
Is there a discotheque in town?	Er det et diskotek her i byen?	ǣr dāy eht diskoot**āyk** hǣr ee bēw̄ern
There's a dance at the...	Det er dans på...	dāy ǣr dahnss paw
Would you like to dance?	Vil De danse?	vil dee **dahnsser**
Yes, I'd love to.	Jo, det vil jeg gjerne.	yoo dāy vil yay y**ǣr**'ner
May I have this dance?	Kan jeg få denne dansen?	kahn yay faw **dehn**ner **dahnss**ern

Do you happen to play...?

On a rainy day, this page may solve your problems.

Do you happen to play chess?	De spiller vel ikke tilfeldigvis sjakk?	dee **spill**err vehl **ikk**er tilfehl**dig**veess shahk
I'm afraid I don't.	Dessverre gjør jeg ikke det.	dehss**vehr**rer yūr yay **ikk**er dāy
No, but I'll give you a game of draughts (checkers).	Nei, men jeg kan spille dam.	nay mehn yay kahn **spill**er dahm
king	konge	**kong**er
queen	dronning	**dronn**ing
castle (rook)	tårn	taw'n
bishop	løper	**lūr**perr
knight	springer	**spring**err
pawn	bonde	**boonn**er
Check!	Sjakk!	shahk
Checkmate!	Sjakk matt!	shahk maht
Do you play cards?	Spiller De kort?	**spill**err dee ko't
bridge	bridge	bridsh
canasta	canasta	kah**nahss**tah
gin rummy	gin rummy	jin **rurm**mi
whist	whist	visst
pontoon (21)	21	khēw̄er-āyn
poker	poker	**poō**kerr

ace	ess	ehss
king	konge	konger
queen	dronning	dronning
jack	knekt	knehkt
joker	joker	yōōkerr
hearts	hjerter	yæ'terr
diamonds	ruter	rēwterr
clubs	kløver	klūrverr
spades	spar	spaar

Gambling

There are no casinos in Norway. The number of ways you can gamble is limited. But if you must, try:

Football pools *(tipping)*. Wednesday at 5 p.m. is the deadline for picking the results of 12 matches. In summer the bets are mostly on Norwegian teams, otherwise British clubs are represented.

Horse racing. Where there are horses there are bound to be gamblers; thoroughbred and harness racing is held at several race-courses.

Lottery. Playing the numbers is legal in Norway. See your nearest bank or tobacco shop, though your own hunch number may not be available when and where you want. *Det norske Pengelotteri* is drawn on the 10th of each month.

Bingo is an import of recent years that will need no explanation to Britons or Americans. It has spread to countless towns and villages throughout the length and breadth of the country.

FOR NUMBERS, see page 175

Sports

During the summer season you have your choice of swimming in the sea, in rivers or in open-air swimming pools. Around Oslo you will have to pay at official bathing places. Unfortunately, Oslo Fjord is not noted for the purity of its water. But along the south coast of Norway you can find many beautiful islands and small bays with rocky or sandy beaches. This is where the Norwegians themselves go on holiday; the water here is beautiful.

Where's the nearest golf course?	Hvor ligger nærmeste golfbane?	voor liggerr nærmehsster golfbaaner
Can we hire (rent) clubs?	Kan vi leie køller?	kahn vee layer kurller
Where are the tennis courts?	Hvor finnes det tennisbaner?	voor finners day tehnnissbaanerr
Can I hire rackets?	Kan jeg leie racketer?	kahn yay layer rahkehtterr
What's the charge per...?	Hva koster det pr...?	vah kossterr day pær
day	dag	daag
round	omgang	omgahng
hour	time	teemer
Where's the nearest race-course?	Hvor er nærmeste veddeløpsbane?	voor ær nærmehsster vehdderlurpssbaaner
What's the admission charge?	Hva koster det å komme inn?	vah kossterr day aw kommer in
Is there a swimming pool here?	Er det et svømme-basseng her?	ær day eht svurmmer-bahssehng hær
Is it open-air or indoors?	Er det frilufts- eller innendørs-basseng?	ær day freelewfts-ehllerr innerndursh-bahssehng
Is it heated?	Er det oppvarmet?	ær day opvahrmet
Can one swim in the lake/river?	Kan man bade i innsjøen/elven?	kahn mahn baader ee inshūern/ehlvern
Is there a bowling alley/billard hall near here?	Finnes det en bowling-hall/et biljard-rom i nærheten?	finners day ehn bowling-hahl/eht bilyah'd-room ee nærhehtern

RELAXING

I'd like to see a boxing/wrestling match.	Jeg vil gjerne se en bokse-/bryte- kamp.	yay vil yǽ'rner sāy ehn bokser/brēwter- kahmp
Can you get 2 tickets?	Kan De skaffe 2 billetter?	kahn dee skahffer 2 billehtterr
Is there a football (soccer) match any- where this Saturday?	Spilles det en fot- ballkamp i nærheten på lørdag?	spillers dāy ehn foot- bahlkahmp ee nǽrhehtern paw lūr'daag
Who is playing?	Hvem spiller?	vehm spillerr
Is there any good fishing around here?	Finnes det noen fine fiskeplasser i nærheten?	finners dāy nōōern feener fiskerplahsserr ee nǽrhehtern
Do I need a permit?	Må jeg ha til- latelse?	maw yay haa tillaaterlsser
Where can I get one?	Hvor kan jeg få det?	voor kahn yay faw dāy

RELAXING

Fishing

More than 200 Norwegian rivers are jumping with salmon and trout. The season extends from June to September. To reserve fishing rights, check with a travel agency in advance.

The best trout fishing is to be found in the mountains, well off the beaten track. Taxi-plane companies organize expeditions.

You'll need a fishing permit (*fiskekort*—**fisk**erko'rt), of course. The cost varies with the location. These permits are often sold in hotels, tourist information offices, travel agen- cies...and even in food shops.

On the beach

Is it safe for swimming?	Er det trygt å svømme her?	ǣr dāy trewgt aw svurmmer hǣr
Is there a lifeguard?	Finnes det en livredder?	finnerss dāy ehn leevrehdderr
Is it safe for children?	Er det trygt for barn?	ǣr dāy trewgt for baa'n

It's very calm.	**Det er veldig stille.**	dāy ær **vehl**di stiller
There are some big waves.	**Det er noen store bølger.**	dāy ær **nōō**ern **stōō**rer burlgerr
Is it a good place for snorkelling?	**Er det et bra sted å dykke?**	ær dāy eht braa stāyd aw **dewk**ker
Are there any dangerous currents?	**Er det noen farlige strømmer?**	ær dāy **nōō**ern **faar**leeer **strurm**merr
What time is high/low tide?	**Når er det høy-/lav-vann?**	nawr ær dāy hoy-/laav-vahn
What's the temperature of the water?	**Hvor mange grader er det i vannet?**	voor **mahng**er **graad**err ær dāy ee **vahn**ner
I want to hire a/an/some...	**Jeg vil gjerne leie...**	yay vil **yǣr**ner **lay**er
air-mattress	**en luftmadrass**	ehn **lewft**mahdrahss
bath towel	**et badehåndkle**	eht **baad**erhawnklāy
bathing hut	**et badehus**	eht **baad**erhewss
bathing suit	**en badedrakt**	ehn **baad**erdrahkt
deck-chair	**en liggestol**	ehn **ligg**ersstōōl
skin-diving equipment	**dykkerutstyr**	**dewk**kehrewtstewr
sunshade	**en parasoll**	ehn **pah**rahssol
surfboard	**et brett til surfriding**	eht breht til **sūrf**frayding
swimming belt	**et svømmebelte**	eht **svurm**merbehlter
tent	**et telt**	eht tehlt
water-skis	**et par vannski**	eht paar **vahn**shee
Where can I rent a...?	**Hvor kan jeg leie en...?**	voor kahn yay **lay**er ehn
canoe	**kano**	**kaa**noo
kayak	**kajakk**	**kah**yahk
motor boat	**motorbåt**	**mōō**toorbawt
rowing-boat	**robåt**	**rōō**bawt
sailing-boat	**seilbåt**	**sayl**bawt
What's the charge per hour?	**Hva koster det pr. time?**	vah **koss**terr dāy pær **tee**mer

PRIVAT STRAND
PRIVATE BEACH

FORBUDT Å BADE
NO BATHING

Winter sports

Skiing is Norway's national sport. The season in Oslo—one of the world's ski capitals—lasts from late December till late March. But above 3,500 feet skiing continues into May.

Though most Norwegians are cross-country ski enthusiasts, the trend now is towards slalom and downhill skiing (*ut-for*—~~ewt~~for).

Skating is the second most popular winter sport. It starts before the skiing season, when the lakes freeze. Most towns have open-air rinks.

Is there a skating-rink near here?	**Finnes det en skøyte-bane i nærheten?**	finners dāy ehn **shoyter**-baaner ee **nǣr**hehtern
What are the skiing conditions like at Lillehammer?	**Hvordan er skifor-holdene på Lille-hammer?**	voo'dahn **ǣr** sheefor-holderner paw **liller**-hahmmerr
Can I take skiing lessons there?	**Kan jeg få skiunder-visning der?**	kahn yay faw **shee**ewnnehr-veessning **dǣr**
Are there any ski lifts?	**Finnes det skiheiser?**	finners dāy **shee**haysserr
Where's there a good place for cross-country skiing?	**Hvor er det fint å gå på tur-langrenn?**	voor **ǣr** dāy feent aw gaw paw **tēwr**-lahngrehn
I want to hire/buy a/some...	**Jeg vil gjerne leie/kjøpe...**	yay vil **yǣ**'ner layer/**khūr**per
cross-country skis	**et par langrennsski**	eht paar **lahng**rehnsshee
ice skates	**et par skøyter**	eht paar **shoyter**r
ski bindings	**bindinger**	**bindinger**r
ski boots	**et par skistøvler**	eht paar **shee**sturvlerr
ski poles	**et par skistaver**	eht paar **shee**staaverr
ski wax	**skismøring**	**shee**smūrring
skiing equipment	**skiutstyr**	**shee**ewtstewr
skis	**et par ski**	eht paar shee
sled	**en slede**	ehn **slāy**der
toboggan	**en kjelke**	ehn **kheh**lker

RELAXING

Camping—Countryside

Of the 1200 authorized camping sites in Norway, about 500 are run by the Norwegian Automobile Association (NAF). The Royal Automobile Club (KNA) runs others, and the rest are operated by other organizations, municipalities or private owners. Camping sites are divided into three categories:

> **Three stars:** very well appointed
> **Two stars:** well appointed
> **One star:** adequate

Many sites are equipped with cabins (*campinghytter*—**kæm**-ping**hewt**terr). A typical cabin, equipped with mattresses only, can accommodate four persons.

If you want to camp on private land, get permission from the owner first.

Can we camp here?	**Kan vi campe her?**	kahn vee **kæm**per h**æ**r
Is there a camping site near here?	**Finnes det en campingplass i nærheten?**	finners d$\overline{\text{ay}}$ ehn **kæm**ping-plahss ee n**æ**rhehtern
May we camp in your field?	**Kan vi slå opp teltet på jordet Deres?**	kahn vee slaw op **tehl**ter paw y$\overline{\text{oo}}$rer d**ay**rerss
Can we park our caravan (trailer) here?	**Kan vi sette campingvognen her?**	kahn vee **seht**ter **kæm**pingvongnern h**æ**r
Is drinking water available?	**Finnes det drikkevann?**	finners d$\overline{\text{ay}}$ **drikk**er-vahn
Are there...?	**Er det...?**	$\overline{\text{æ}}$r d$\overline{\text{ay}}$
baths	**bad**	baad
showers	**dusj**	dewsh
toilets	**toalett**	tooah**leht**

DRIKKEVANN	**FORURENSET VANN**
DRINKING WATER	POLLUTED WATER

What's the charge...?	Hva koster det...?	vah **kosst**err day
per day	**pr. dag**	pær daag
per person	**pr. person**	pær pæshoon
for a car	**for en bil**	for ehn beel
for a tent	**for et telt**	for eht tehlt
for a caravan (trailer)	**for en campingvogn**	for ehn **kæm**pingvongn
Is there a youth hostel near here?	**Er det et ungdoms-herberge i nær-heten?**	ær day eht **oong**doms-**hæær**bæærger ee n**æær**hehtern
Do you know anyone who can put us up for the night?	**Kjenner De noen som kan gi oss husly for natten?**	**kheh**nnerr dee nooern som kahn yee oss **hewss**lew for **naht**tern

CAMPING FORBUDT	CAMPINGVOGNER FORBUDT
NO CAMPING	NO CARAVANS (TRAILERS)

CAMPING–COUNTRYSIDE

Landmarks

barn	**låve**	**law**ver
boulder	**kampestein**	**kahm**perstayn
bridge	**bro**	broo
brook	**bekk**	behk
building	**bygning**	**bewg**ning
canal	**kanal**	kah**naal**
castle	**slott**	slot
chapel	**kapell**	kah**pehl**
church	**kirke**	**kheer**ker
cliff	**klippe**	**klip**per
copse	**småskog**	smawskoog
cottage	**hytte**	**hewt**ter
crossroads	**korsvei**	**ko'ss**vay
farm	**bondegård**	**boon**nergawr
ferry	**ferge**	**fær**ger
field	**mark**	mahrk
footpath	**sti**	stee
forest	**skog**	skoog
fork in the road	**skillevei**	**shil**lervay
gorge	**kløft**	klurft
grove	**lund**	lewnn
heath	**hei**	hay
highway	**landevei**	**lahn**nervay
hill	**ås**	awss

house	hus	hewss
inn	vertshus	væ'rtshewss
lake	innsjø	inshūr
marsh	myr	mewr
moorland	lyngmo	lewngmoo
mountain	fjell	fyehl
mountain range	fjellkjede	fyehlkhāyder
path	sti	stee
peak	topp	top
pond	dam	dahm
pool	kulp	kewlp
railway	jernbane	yǣ'nbaaner
ravine	kløft	klurft
river	elv	ehlv
road	vei	vay
ruin	ruiner	reweenerr
sea	sjø	shūr
spring	kilde	khilder
stream	bekk	behk
swamp	sump	soomp
tower	tårn	taw'n
track	spor	spōor
tree	tre	trāy
tunnel	tunnel	tewnnehl
valley	dal	daal
village	landsby	lahndssbew
waterfall	foss	foss
well	brønn	brurn
wood	skog	skōog

UVEDKOMMENDE FORBUDT

NO TRESPASSING

| What's the name of that river? | Hva heter den elven der? | vah hāyter dehn ehlven dǣr |
| How high is that mountain? | Hvor høyt er det fjellet der? | voor hoyt ǣr dāy fyehller dǣr |

...and if you're tired of walking, you can always try hitch-hiking—though you may have to wait a long time for a lift.

| Can you give me a lift to...? | Kan jeg få sitte på til...? | kahn yay faw sitter paw til |

FOR ASKING THE WAY, see page 144

Making friends

Norway is sometimes said to be a nation of contemplative people. So don't expect a conversation to start up spontaneously.

Introductions

How do you do?	God dag.*	goo daag
Very well, thank you.	Bra, takk.	braa tahk
Fine, thanks. And you?	Fint, takk. Hvordan har De det?	feent tahk. voo'dahn haar dee day
May I introduce Miss Hansen.	Får jeg presentere frøken Hansen.	fawr yay prehssangtayrer frūrkern hahnssern
I'd like you to meet a friend of mine.	Jeg vil gjerne De skal møte en venn av meg.	yay vil yǣ'ner dee skahl mūrter ehn vehn ahv may
Bob, this is...	Bob, dette er...	bob dehtter ær
My name's...	Mitt navn er...	mit nahvn ær
Glad to know you.	Hyggelig å hilse på Dem.	hewggerli aw hilsser paw dehm

Follow-up

How long have you been here?	Hvor lenge har De vært her?	voor lehnger haar dee vǣ't hǣr
We've been here a week.	Vi har vært her en uke.	vee haar vǣ't hǣr ehn ēwker
Is this your first visit?	Er det første gang De er her?	ær day furshter gahng dee ær hǣr
No, we came here last year.	Nei, vi var her i fjor.	nay vee vaar hǣr ee fyōor
Are you enjoying your stay?	Liker De Dem her?	leekerr dee dehm hǣr
Yes, I like...very much.	Ja, jeg synes at det er veldig bra i...	yah yay sēwnerss aht day ær vehldi braa ee
Are you on your own?	Er De alene her?	ær dee ahlāyner hǣr

* This is the normal response when introduced to someone.

I'm with...	Jeg er sammen med...	yay ær **sahm**mern māy
my husband	min mann	meen mahn
my wife	min kone	meen **kōō**ner
my family	min familie	meen fah**mee**leeer
my parents	mine foreldre	**mee**ner fo**rehl**drer
some friends	noen venner	**nōō**ern **vehn**nerr
Where do you come from?	Hvor kommer De fra?	voor **kom**merr dee fraa
I'm from...	Jeg kommer fra...	yay **kom**merr fraa
Where are you staying?	Hvor bor De?	voor bōōr dee
We're here on holiday.	Vi er her på ferie.	vee ær hær paw **fāy**reeer
I'm here on business.	Jeg er her i forret- ninger.	yay ær hær ee for**reht**ningerr
What kind of business are you in?	Hvilke forretninger driver De med?	**vil**ker for**reht**ningerr **dree**verr dee māy
I hope we'll see you again soon.	Jeg håper vi ses igjen snart.	yay **haw**perr vee **sāy**ss ee**yehn** snaa't
See you later/See you tomorrow.	Ser Dem senere/ Ser Dem i morgen.	sāyr dehm **sāy**nehrer/ sāyr dehm ee **maw**ern

The weather

Always a good topic for conversation, in Norway as else-where.

What a lovely day!	For en skjønn dag!	for ehn shurn daag
What awful weather!	For et fryktelig vær!	for eht **frewk**terli vær
Is it usually as warm/ cool as this?	Er det vanligvis så varmt/kaldt som dette?	ær dāy **vaan**liveess saw vahrmt/kahlt som **deht**ter
Do you think it'll... tomorrow?	Tror De at det vil...i morgen?	trōōr dee aht dāy vil...ee **maw**ern
rain/snow	regne/snø	**ray**ner/snūr
clear up/be sunny	klarne opp/bli sol	**klaa'**ner op/blee sool
What's the weather forecast?	Hvordan er vær-meldingen?	**voo'**dahn ær vær-**mehl**dingern

Invitations

My wife and I would like you to dine with us on...	Min kone og jeg vil gjerne at De skal spise middag med oss...	meen **kōō**ner o yay vil **yāō**rner aht dee skahl **speess**er middaag māy oss
Can you come to dinner tomorrow night?	Kan De komme til middag i morgen kveld?	kahn dee **kom**mer til **midd**aag ee **maw**ern kvehl
Can you join us for a drink this evening?	Kunne De tenke Dem å ta en drink sammen med oss i kveld?	**kewn**ner dee **tehn**ker dehm aw taa ehn drink **sahm**mern māy oss ee kvehl
There's a party. Are you coming?	Det er selskap. Kommer De?	dāy **ǣr sehl**skaap. **kom**merr dee
That's very kind of you.	Det er veldig hyggelig av Dem.	dāy **ǣr vehl**di **hewg**gerli ahv dehm
What time shall we come?	Når skal vi komme?	nawr skahl vee **kom**mer
May I bring a friend?	Kan jeg få ta med en venn?	kahn yay faw taa māy ehn vehn
I'm afraid we've got to go now.	Jeg er lei for at vi må gå nå.	yay **ǣr** lay for aht vee maw gaw naw
Thanks for the evening. It was great.	Takk for i kveld. Det var veldig hyggelig.	tahk for ee kvehl. dāy vaar **vehl**di **hewg**gerli

Dating

Would you like a cigarette?	Vil De* ha en sigarett?	vil dee haa ehn **sigg**ah**reht**
Do you have a light, please?	Unnskyld, har De fyr?	**ewn**shewl, haar dee fēwr
Can I get you a drink?	Kan jeg skaffe Dem en drink?	kahn yay **skahf**fer dehm ehn drink
Excuse me, could you please help me?	Unnskyld, men kunne De hjelpe meg?	**ewn**shewl, mehn **kewn**ner dee **yehl**per may
Haven't we met somewhere before?	Har ikke vi møtt hverandre før?	haar **ik**ker vee murt **veh**randrer fūrr

MAKING FRIENDS

* For ease of reading we give only the formal form of address (**De/Dem**) here. You'll quickly graduate to the more informal **du/deg** (dew/day). See page 10 of our "Grammar" section.

96

I'm lost. Can you show me the way to...?	Jeg har gått meg bort. Kan De vise meg veien til...	yay haar got may boo't. kahn dee veesser may vayern til
Are you waiting for someone?	Venter De på noen?	vehnterr dee paw nōōern
Are you free this evening?	Er De ledig i kveld?	ār dee lāydi ee kvehl
Would you like to go out with me tonight?	Kunne De tenke Dem å gå ut med meg i kveld?	kewnner dee tehnker dehm aw gaw ēwt māy may ee kvehl
Would you like to go dancing?	Kunne De tenke Dem å gå ut og danse?	kewnner dee tehnker dehm aw gaw ēwt o dahnsser
I know a good discotheque/restaurant.	Jeg vet om et godt diskotek/en god restaurant.	yay vāyt om eht got diskootāyk/ehn gōō rehsterrahng
Shall we go to the cinema (movies)?	Skal vi gå på kino?	skahl vee gaw paw kheenoo
Would you like to go for a drive?	Kunne De tenke Dem å kjøre en tur?	kewnner dee tehnker dehm aw khūrrer ehn tēwr
Where shall we meet?	Hvor skal vi møtes?	voor skahl vee mūrterss
I'll pick you up at your hotel.	Jeg henter Dem på hotellet Deres.*	yay hehnterr dehm paw hootehller dāyrerss*
I'll call for you at 8.	Jeg kommer klokken 8.	yay kommerr klokkern 8
May I take you home?	Kan jeg få følge Dem hjem?	kahn yay faw furller dehm yehm
Can I see you again tomorrow?	Kan jeg få treffe Dem i morgen?	kahn yay faw trehffer dehm ee mawern
Thank you, it's been a wonderful evening.	Tusen takk. Det har vært en veldig hygge-lig kveld.	tēwssern tahk. dāy haar vā''t ehn vehldi hewggerli kvehl
What's your telephone number?	Hva er telefon-nummeret Deres?*	vah ār tehlehfōōn-noommehrer dāyrerss*
Do you live with your family?	Bor De sammen med familien Deres?**	bōōr dee sahmmern māy fameeleeern dāyrerss**
Do you live alone?	Bor De alene?	bōōr dee ahlāyner
What time is your last bus?	Når går Deres** siste buss?	nawr gawr dāyrerss** sisster bewss

*Informally, **Deres** here becomes **ditt** (dit)
Informally, **Deres here becomes **din** (deen)

MAKING FRIENDS

Shopping guide

This shopping guide is designed to help you find what you want with ease, accuracy and speed. It features:

1. A list of all major types of shops and services (page 98)
2. Some general expressions useful when shopping to allow you to define your requirements precisely (page 100)
3. Full details of the shops and services likely to concern you. Here you'll find advice, phrases, alphabetical lists of items and conversion charts listed under the headings below.

		Page
Bookshop	reading matter, stationery, authors	104
Camping	camping equipment, crockery, cutlery	106
Chemist's (drugstore)	medicine, first-aid, toilet articles	108
Clothing	clothes, shoes, accessories, material, colours, clothing sizes	112
Electrical appliances	radios, tape-recorders, shavers, records	119
Hairdresser's	barber's, ladies' hairdresser's	121
Jeweller's	watches, repairs, jewellery	123
Laundry— Dry-cleaning	usual facilities	126
Photography	film, processing, accessories, repairs	127
Provisions	what you'll want to buy for a picnic	130
Souvenirs	souvenirs, gifts	132
Tobacconist's	smoker's supplies	133

Shops, Stores and Services

From Monday to Friday most shops remain open from 9 a.m. to 5 p.m. without a break for lunch. On Saturday the opening hours are from 9 a.m. to 2 p.m.

Haggling, in shops or at the market, is simply not done in Norway.

Where's the nearest...?	Hvor er nærmeste...?	voor ær nærmehsster
antique shop	antikvitetshandel	ahntikvitaytshahnderl
art gallery	kunstgalleri	kewnsstgahllerree
bakery	baker	baakerr
bank	bank	bahnk
barber	herrefrisør	hærrerfrissurr
beauty salon	skjønnhetssalong	shurnhaytssahlong
bookshop	bokhandel	bookhahnderl
bookstall	bok-kiosk	book-khiosk
bootblack	skopusser	skoopewsserr
butcher	slakter	slahkterr
cable office	telegrafkontor	tehlehgraaf-koontoor
camera store	fotoforretning	footoo-forrehtning
candy store	sjokoladeforretning	shookoolaaderforrehtning
chemist	apotek	ahpootayk
cigar store	sigarforretning	siggaarforrehtning
cigarette stand	sigarett-automat	siggahreht-owtoomaat
cobbler	skomaker	skoomaakerr
confectioner	konditor	koonditoor
dairy	meieri	mayehree
delicatessen	delikatesseforretning	dehlikahtehsserforrehtning
dentist	tannlege	tahnlayger
department store	stormagasin	stoormahgahsseen
doctor	lege	layger
draper	manufaktur	mahnewfahktewr
dressmaker	dameskredder	daamerskrehdderr
drugstore	apotek	ahpootayk
dry-cleaner	renseri	rehnssehree
dry-goods store	manufaktur	mahnewfahktewr
filling station	bensinstasjon	behnsseenstashoon
fishmonger	fiskehandel	fiskerhahnderl
flea-market	loppemarked	loppermahrkerd
florist	blomsterforretning	bloomsterrforrehtning
furrier	pelsforretning	pehlssforrehtning

garage	bilverksted	beelværkstay
greengrocer	grønnsakshandel	grurnssaaksshahnderl
grocery	kolonialhandel	koolooniaalhahnderl
hairdresser (ladies)	damefrisør	daamerfrissurr
hardware store	jernvarehandel	yaͤrnvaarerhahnderl
hat shop	hatteforretning	hahtterforrehtning
health-food shop	helsekostforretning	hehlsserkosst-forrehtning
hospital	hospital	hoospitaal
ironmonger	jernvarehandel	yaͤrnvaarerhahnderl
jeweller	gullsmed	gewllsmay
launderette	selvbetjenings-vaskeri	sehlbertyayningss-vahskerree
laundry	vaskeri	vahskerree
leather-goods store	lærvareforretning	laͤrvaarerforrehtning
liquor store	vinmonopol	veenmoonoopool
market	torg	torg
milliner	hattemagasin	hahttermahgahsseen
newsagent	avisselger	ahveessehlgerr
news-stand	aviskiosk	ahveesskhiosk
optician	optiker	optikerr
pastry shop	konditori	koonditooree
pawnbroker	pantelåner	pahnterlawnerr
petrol station	bensinstasjon	behnsseenstahshoon
photographer	fotograf	footoograaf
photo shop	fotoforretning	footoo-forrehtning
police station	politistasjon	pooliteestahshoon
post-office	postkontor	posstkoontoor
shirt-maker	skjorteforretning	shoorterforrehtning
shoemaker (repairs)	skomaker	skoomaakerr
shoe shop	skoforretning	skoo-forrehtning
souvenir shop	souvenirbutikk	sewvehneer-bewtik
sporting-goods shop	sportsforretning	sportsforrehtning
stationer	papirhandel	pahpeerhahnderl
supermarket	supermarked	sewpehrmahrkerd
sweet-shop	sjokoladeforretning	shookoolaaderforrehtning
tailor	skredder	skrehdderr
tea shop	te-forretning	teh-forrehtning
telegraph office	telegraf	tehlehgraaf
tobacconist	tobakksforretning	toobahksforrehtning
toiletry shop	parfymeri	pahrfewmehree
toy shop	leketøysforretning	laykertoysforrehtning
travel agent	reisebyrå	raysserbewraw
vegetable store	grønnsakshandel	grurnssaaksshahnderl
veterinarian	dyrlege	dewrlayger
watchmaker	urmaker	ewrmaakerr
wine merchant	vinmonopol	veenmoonoopool

General expressions

Here are some expressions which will be useful to you when you're out shopping:

Where?

Where's a good...?	Hvor finnes en god...?	voor finners ehn gōō
Where can I find a...?	Hvor kan jeg finne en...?	voor kahn yay finner ehn
Where do they sell...?	Hvor selger de...?	voor sehllerr dee
Can you recommend an inexpensive...?	Kan De anbefale en rimelig...?	kahn dee ahnbehfaaler ehn reemerli
Where's the main shopping area?	Hvor ligger forretningsstrøket?	voor liggerr forrehtningsstrūrker
How far is it from here?	Hvor langt er det herfra?	voor lahngt ær dāy hærfrah
How do I get there?	Hvordan kommer jeg dit?	voo'dahn kommerr yay deet

Service

Can you help me?	Kan De hjelpe meg?	kahn dee yehlper may
I'm just looking around.	Jeg bare ser meg omkring.	yay baarer sāyr may omkring
I want...	Jeg vil gjerne ha...	yay vil yǣ'ner haa
Do you have any...?	Har De noe...?	haar dee nōōer

That one

Can you show me...?	Kan De vise meg...?	kahn dee veesser may
that/those	den der/de der	dehn dǣr/dee dǣr
the one in the window	den som er i vinduet	dehn som ǣr ee vindewer
the one in the display case	den som er i utstillingsmontren	dehn som ǣr ee ēwtstillingssmontrern
It's over there.	Det er der borte.	dāy ǣr dǣr boo'ter

TILBUD SPECIAL OFFER	GODTKJØP BARGAIN	SALG SALES

Defining the article

I'd like a...	**Jeg vil gjerne ha en...**	yay vil **yǣ'**ner haa ehn
I want a...one.	**Jeg vil ha en...en.**	yay vil haa ehn...ehn
big	**stor**	stōor
coloured	**farget**	**fahr**gert
dark	**mørk**	murrk
good	**god**	gōo
large	**stor**	stōor
light (weight)	**lett**	leht
light (colour)	**lys**	lēwss
long	**lang**	lahng
modern	**moderne**	mood**ǣ'**ner
natural	**naturlig**	naht**ēw'**li
oval	**oval**	oo**vaal**
rectangular	**rektangulær**	rehktahngewl**ǣr**
round	**rund**	rewn
short	**kort**	ko't
small	**liten**	**lee**tern
soft	**bløt**	blūrt
square	**firkantet**	**feer**kahntert
sturdy	**kraftig**	**krahf**ti
I don't want anything too expensive.	**Jeg vil ikke ha noe altfor dyrt.**	yay vil **ikker** haa **nōo**er ahltfor dēwrt

Preference

Can you show me some more?	**Kan De vise meg noe mer?**	kahn dee **vees**ser may **nōo**er māyr
Haven't you anything...?	**De har ikke noe...?**	dee haar **ikker** **nōo**er
cheaper/better	**billigere/bedre**	**billeeeh**rer/**bāyd**rer
larger/smaller	**større/mindre**	**stur**rer/**mind**rer

How much?

How much is it?	**Hva koster det?**	vah **koss**terr dāy
I don't understand.	**Jeg forstår ikke.**	yay fo**shtawr ik**ker
Please write it down.	**Vær så snill å skrive det ned.**	vǣr saw snil aw **skree**ver dāy nāyd
I don't want to spend more than...crowns.	**Jeg vil ikke bruke mer enn...kroner.**	yay vil **ikker** br**ēw**ker māyr ehn...**krōo**nerr

FOR COLOURS, see page 113

Decision

That's just what I want.	Det er akkurat det jeg ville ha.	dāy ǣr ahkewraat dāy yay viller haa
It's not quite what I want.	Det er ikke akkurat det jeg ville ha.	dāy ǣr ikker ahkewraat dāy yay viller haa
No, I don't like it.	Nei, jeg liker den ikke.	nay yay leekerr dehn ikker
I'll take it.	Jeg tar den.	yay taar dehn

Ordering

Can you order it for me?	Kan De bestille den til meg?	kahn dee berstiller dehn til may
How long will it take?	Hvor lang tid kommer det til å ta?	voor lahng teed kommerr dāy til aw taa
Will I have any difficulty with customs?	Kan jeg få vanskeligheter med tollen?	kahn yay faw vahnskerlihehterr māy tollern

Delivery

I'll take it with me.	Jeg tar den med meg.	yay taar dehn māy may
Deliver it to the...Hotel.	Vil De bringe den til...hotell?	vil dee bringer dehn til...hootehl
Please send it to this address.	Vil De sende det til denne adressen.	vil dee sehnner dāy til dehnner ahdrehssern

Paying

How much is it?	Hva koster det?	vah kossterr dāy
Can I pay by traveller's cheque?	Kan jeg betale med reisesjekk?	kahn yay bertaaler māy raysser-shehk
Do you accept dollars/pounds/credit cards?	Tar De imot dollar/pund/kredittkort?	taar dee eemōōt dollahr/pewn/krehditko°t
Haven't you made a mistake in the bill?	Har De ikke gjort en feil på regningen?	haar dee ikker yoo°t ehn fayl paw rayningern
Can I please have a receipt?	Kan jeg få en kvittering?	kahn yay faw ehn kvittāyring
Will you please (gift-)wrap it?	Vil De pakke den inn (som presang)?	vil dee pahkker dehn in (som prehssahng)

SHOPPING-GUIDE

Anything else?

No, thanks, that's all.	**Nei takk, det var alt.**	nay tahk dāy vaar ahlt
Yes, I want...	**Ja, jeg vil gjerne ha...**	yah yay vil yǣ'ner haa
Show me...	**Vil De vise meg...?**	vil dee **vees**ser may
Thank you. Good-bye.	**Tusen takk. Adjø.**	**tēw**ssern tahk. ahd**yūr**

Dissatisfied

Can you please exchange this?	**Kan De bytte denne?**	kahn dee **bewt**ter **dehn**ner
I want to return this.	**Jeg vil gjerne levere tilbake denne.**	yay vil yǣ'ner leh**vāy**rer til**baak**er **dehn**ner
I'd like a refund. Here's the receipt.	**Jeg vil gjerne ha det refundert. Her er kvitteringen.**	yay vil yǣ'ner haa dāy rehfewn**day't**. hǣr ǣr kvitt**āy**ringern

Kan jeg hjelpe Dem?	Can I help you?
Hva ønsker De?	What would you like?
Hvilken...kunne De tenke Dem?	What...would you like?
farge/størrelse kvalitet/mengde	colour/shape quality/quantity
Dessverre har vi ikke det.	I'm sorry, we haven't any.
Vi er utsolgt.	We're out of stock.
Skal vi bestille det for Dem?	Shall we order it for you?
Vil De ta det med Dem, eller skal vi sende det?	Will you take it with you or shall we send it?
Var det noe annet?	Anything else?
Det blir...kroner, takk.	That's...crowns, please.
Kassen er der borte.	The cashier's over there.

Bookshop—Stationer's—News-stand

In Norway bookshops and stationers' are usually one and the same shop. Newspapers and magazines are sold at *narvesen-kiosker* (**nahr**vehssernkhio**sk**err) or newsstands. Usually, leading foreign newspapers are on sale. Norway's principal paper, *Aftenposten* (**ahf**tehnposstern) is published daily in Oslo.

Where's the nearest...	**Hvor er nærmeste...?**	voor ær **nær**mehsster
bookshop	**bokhandel**	**boo**khahnderl
stationer's	**papirhandel**	pah**peer**hahnderl
news-stand	**aviskiosk**	ah**veess**khiosk
Can you recommend a good bookshop?	**Kan De anbefale en god bokhandel?**	kahn dee **ahn**behfaaler ehn goo **boo**khahnderl
Where can I buy an English newspaper?	**Hvor kan jeg kjøpe en engelsk avis?**	voor kahn yay **khur**per ehn **ehn**gerlsk ah**veess**
I want to buy a/an/some...	**Jeg vil gjerne kjøpe...**	yay vil **yær**ner **khur**per
address book	**en adressebok**	ehn ah**dreh**sser**boo**k
ball-point pen	**en kulepenn**	ehn **kew**lerpehn
blotting paper	**et trekkpapir**	eht **trehk**pahpeer
book	**en bok**	ehn **boo**k
box of paints	**et malerskrin**	eht **maa**lehrss**k**reen
carbon paper	**karbonpapir**	kahr**boo**npahpeer
cellophane tape	**limbånd**	**leem**bon
crayons	**tegnekritt**	**tay**nerkrit
dictionary	**en ordbok**	ehn **oor**boo**k**
Norwegian/English	**norsk/engelsk**	noshk/**ehn**gerlsk
English/Norwegian	**engelsk/norsk**	**ehn**gerlsk/noshk
pocket dictionary	**en lommeordbok**	ehn **loom**mer**oor**boo**k**
drawing paper	**tegnepapir**	**tay**nerpahpeer
envelopes	**noen konvolutter**	**noo**ern koonvoo**lew**tterr
eraser	**et viskelær**	eht **viss**ker**lær**
exercise book	**en skrivebok**	ehn **skree**ver**boo**k
file	**en brevordner**	ehn **bræ**vordnerr
fountain pen	**en fyllepenn**	ehn **fewl**lerpehn
glue	**noe lim**	**noo**er leem
grammar book	**en grammatikk**	ehn grah**mah**tik
guide book	**en guidebok**	ehn **gayd**-boo**k**
ink	**blekk**	blehk
black/red/blue	**svart/rødt/blått**	svah't/rurt/blawt
magazine	**et blad**	eht blaad

map	et kart	eht kah't
map of the town	et kart over byen	eht kah't **aww**err **bew**ern
road map of...	et veikart over...	eht **vayk**ah't **aww**err
newspaper	en avis	ehn ah**veess**
American	amerikansk	ahmehri**kaansk**
English	engelsk	**ehng**erlsk
notebook	en notisbok	ehn noo**teess**book
notepaper	noe brevpapir	**noo**er **bray**vpahpeer
paperback	en pocketbok	ehn pokkert**book**
paper napkins	noen papirservietter	**noo**ern pahpeers**ær**-vyehtterr
paste	lim	leem
pen	en penn	ehn pehn
pencil	en blyant	ehn **blew**ahnt
pencil sharpener	en blyantspisser	ehn **blew**ahntspisserr
playing cards	en kortstokk	ehn **ko'**tstok
postcards	noen postkort	**noo**ern posst**ko**'t
refill (for a pen)	en refill (til en penn)	ehn reh**fill** (til ehn pehn)
rubber	et viskelær	eht **viss**kerlær
ruler	en linjal	ehn lin**yaal**
sketching block	en skisseblokk	ehn **shiss**erblok
string	hyssing	**hew**ssing
tissue paper	papirlommetørklær	pahpeerloommerturrk**lær**r
tracing paper	noen kalkerpapir	**noo**ern kahl**kay**rpahpeer
typewriter ribbon	fargebånd til maskin	**fahr**gerbon til mah**sheen**
typing paper	skrivemaskinpapir	**skreev**ermasheenpahpeer
wrapping paper	innpakningspapir	**in**pahkningsspahpeer
writing pad	en skriveblokk	ehn **skree**verblok
Where's the guide-book section?	Hvor er avdelingen for guidebøker?	voor **ær** ahv**day**lingern for **gayd**-burkerr
Where do you keep the English books?	Hvor har De engelske bøker?	voor haar dee **ehng**erlske **bur**kerr
Have you any of...'s books in English?	Har De noen av...s bøker på engelsk?	haar dee **noo**ern ahv...s **bur**kerr paw **ehng**erlsk
Is there an English translation of...?	Finnes det en engelsk oversettelse av...?	finners **day** ehn **ehng**erlsk **aww**verrssehtterlsser ahv

SHOPPING-GUIDE

The famous Norwegian writers Henrik Ibsen and Knut Hamsun have been translated into English with many works available in paperback. But you will discover that few Norwegian writers of today are translated. A best-seller exception is Thor Heyerdahl, whose sea voyages on Kon-Tiki, Ra I and Ra II are known everywhere.

Camping

Here we're concerned with the equipment you may need.

I'd like a/an/some...	Jeg vil gjerne ha...	yay vil yǣ'rner haa
axe	en øks	ehn urks
bottle-opener	en flaskeåpner	ehn **flahss**kerawpnerr
bucket	en bøtte	ehn **burt**ter
butane gas	propangass	proopaangahss
camp bed	en campingseng	ehn **kæm**pingssehng
camping equipment	noe campingutstyr	nōōer **kæm**pingewtsstewr
can opener	en boksåpner	ehn boksawpnerr
candles	noen stearinlys	nōōern stehahreen**lew**ss
chair	en stol	ehn stōōl
folding chair	en sammenleggbar stol	ehn **sahm**mernlehgbahr stōōl
compass	et kompass	eht koom**pahss**
corkscrew	en korketrekker	ehn **kork**ertrehkkerr
crockery	noe stentøy	nōōer **stayn**toy
cutlery	spisebestikk	**spees**serberstik
deck-chair	en fluktstol	ehn **flewkt**stōōl
first-aid kit	noe førstehjelps-utstyr	nōōer furshteryehlpss-ewtsstewr
fishing tackle	noe fiskeredskap	nōōer fiskerrǣydsskaap
flashlight	en lommelykt	ehn **loom**merlewkt
frying-pan	en stekepanne	ehn **stay**kerpahnner
groundsheet	et underlag	eht **ewn**nerrlaag
hammer	en hammer	ehn **hahm**merr
haversack	en skulderveske	ehn **skewl**derrvehssker
ice-bag	en kjølebag	ehn **khūr**lerbæg
kerosene (U.S.)	parafin	pahrah**feen**
kettle	en kjele	ehn **khāy**ler
knapsack	en ransel	ehn **rahn**sserl
lamp	en lampe	ehn **lahm**per
lantern	en lanterne	ehn lahn**tæ**'ner
matches	noen fyrstikker	nōōern **few**shtikkerr
mattress	en madrass	ehn mah**drahss**
methylated spirits	trespirit	**trǣy**spreet
mosquito net	et fluenett	eht **flew**erneht
paraffin (Br.)	parafin	pahrah**feen**
penknife	en pennekniv	ehn **pehn**nerkneev
picnic case	en picnic-kurv	ehn piknik-kewrv
pressure cooker	en trykk-koker	ehn trewk-kōōkerr
primus stove	en primus	ehn **pree**mewss
rope	et tau	eht tow
rucksack	en ryggsekk	ehn **rewg**ssehk
saucepan	en kasserolle	ehn kahss**err**oller

scissors	en saks	ehn sahks
screwdriver	en skrutrekker	ehn skrewtrehkkerr
sheathknife	en slirekniv	ehn sleererkneev
sleeping bag	en sovepose	ehn sawverpoosser
stewpan	en gryte	ehn grewter
stove	en ovn	ehn ovn
table	et bord	eht boor
folding table	et sammenleggbart bord	eht sahmmernlehgbahrt boor
tent	et telt	eht tehlt
tent-pegs	noen teltplugger	nooern tehltplewggerr
tent-pole	en teltstang	ehn tehltstahng
thermos flask (bottle)	en termosflaske	ehn tehrmoossflahssker
tin-opener	en boksåpner	ehn boksawpnerr
tongs	en tang	ehn tahng
tool kit	en verktøykasse	ehn værktoykahsser
torch	en lommelykt	ehn loommerlewkt
wood alcohol	tresprit	trayspreet

Crockery

cups	kopper	kopperr
dishes	fat/tallerkener	faat/tahlærkernerr
food-box	matboks	maatboks
mugs	krus	krewss
plates	tallerkener	tahlærkernerr
saucers	skåler	skawlerr

Cutlery

forks	gafler	gahfflerr
knives	kniver	kneeverr
spoons	skjeer	shayerr
teaspoons	teskjeer	tayshayerr
(made of) plastic	(i) plast	(ee) plahsst
(made of) stainless steel	(i) rustfritt stål	(ee) rewsstfrit stawl

Chemist's—Drugstore

A Norwegian *apotek* (ahpoo**tayk**) doesn't stock the wide range of goods that you'll find in the equivalent shop in Britain or the U.S. For example, they don't sell photographic equipment or books. And for perfume, cosmetics etc. you must go to a *parfymeri* (pahrfewmeh**ree**). In the window of every *apotek* is a notice telling where the nearest all-night service is.

This section has been divided into two parts:

1. Pharmaceutical—medicine, first-aid etc.
2. Toiletry—toilet articles, cosmetics

General

Where's the nearest (all-night) chemist's?	Hvor er nærmeste apotek (med natte-vakt)?	voor **ær** **nær**mehsster ahpoo**tayk** (may nahtter-vahkt)
What time does the chemist's open/close?	Når åpner/stenger apoteket?	nawr **awp**nerr/**stehn**gerr ahpoo**tay**ker

Part 1—Pharmaceutical

I want something for...	Jeg skal ha noe mot...	yay skahl haa **noo**er **moot**
a cold/a cough	forkjølelse/hoste	for**khur**lerlsser/**hoos**ster
hay fever	høysnue	**hoy**snewer
a headache	hodepine	**hoo**derpeener
sunburn	solbrenthet	**sool**brehnt**hayt**
an upset stomach	magesyke	**maag**erssewker
Can you make up this prescription for me?	Kan De gjøre istand det som står på resepten for meg?	kahn dee **yur**rer ee**stahn** day som stawr paw reh**ssehp**tern for may
Shall I wait?	Skal jeg vente?	skahl yay **vehn**ter
When shall I come back?	Når skal jeg komme tilbake?	nawr skahl yay **kom**mer til**baa**ker
Can I get it without a prescription?	Kan jeg få det uten resept?	kahn yay faw day **ew**tern reh**ssehpt**

FOR DOCTOR, see page 162

SHOPPING-GUIDE

Can I have a/an/some...?	Kan jeg få...?	kahn yay faw
antiseptic cream	en antiseptisk salve	ehn ahntisehptisk sahlver
bandage	en bandasje	ehn bahndaasher
Band-Aids	litt plaster	lit plahssterr
calcium tablets	noen kalktabletter	nōoern kahlktahblehtterr
chlorine tablets	noen klortabletter	nōoern klōortahblehtterr
contraceptives	noen preventiver	nōoern prāyvangteeverr
corn plasters	noe liktornplaster	nōoer leektoo'nplahssterr
cotton wool	litt bomull	lit boomewl
cough drops	noen hostepastiller	nōoern hoossterpahsstillerr
diabetic lozenges	noen diabetiker-pastiller	nōoern diahbāytikerr-pahsstillerr
disinfectant	et desinfeksjons-middel	eht dehssinfehkshōons-midderl
ear drops	en flaske øredråper	ehn flahssker ūrrerdrawperr
Elastoplast	litt plaster	lit plahssterr
eye drops	en flaske øyedråper	ehn flahssker oyerdrawperr
first-aid kit	et førstehjelps-utstyr	eht furshteryehlps-ēwtsstewr
gauze	et gasbind	eht gahssbin
insect lotion	et flytende insekt-middel	eht flēwternder inssehktsmidderl
iodine	en flaske jod	ehn flahssker yod
iron pills	noen jernpiller	nōoern yāe'npillerr
laxative	et avføringsmiddel	eht aavfūrringsmidderl
lint	et forbindingsstoff	eht forbinningsstof
mouthwash	et munnvann	eht mewnvahn
quinine tablets	noen kinintabletter	nōoern kineentahblehtterr
sanitary napkins	en pakke sanitets-bind	ehn pahkker sahnitāyts-bin
sleeping pills	noen sovepiller	nōoern sawverpillerr
stomach pills	noen magepiller	nōoern maagerpillerr
surgical dressing	noen forbindings-saker	nōoern forbinnings-saaker
thermometer	et termometer	eht tærmoomāyterr
throat lozenges	noen halspastiller	nōoern hahlsspahsstillerr
tissues	noen servietter	nōoern særvyehtterr
vitamin pills	noen vitaminpiller	nōoern vittahmeenpillerr

GIFT! KUN TIL UTVENDIG BRUK (MÅ IKKE TAS INN)	POISON! FOR EXTERNAL USE ONLY

Part 2—Toiletry

I'd like a/an/some...	Jeg vil gjerne ha...	yay vil y**æ**'ner haa
acne cream	en aknesalve	ehn **ahk**nerssahlver
after-shave lotion	et etterbarberings-vann	eht ehtterrbahrb**ā**yrings-vahn
astringent	et astringerende vann	eht ahsstring**ā**yrehnder vahn
bath salts	et badesalt	eht **baa**derssahlt
cream	en krem	ehn kr**ā**ym
cleansing cream	en rensekrem	ehn **rehn**sserkr**ā**ym
cold cream	en koldkrem	ehn kolkr**ā**ym
cuticle cream	en neglebåndkrem	ehn **nayler**bonkr**ā**ym
foundation cream	en underlagskrem	ehn **ewn**nerrlaagsskr**ā**ym
moisturizing cream	en fuktighetskrem	ehn **fewk**tih**ā**ytskr**ā**ym
night cream	en nattkrem	ehn **naht**kr**ā**ym
cuticle remover	en neglebåndsfjerner	ehn **nayler**bonssfy**ā**'nerr
deodorant	en deodorant	ehn **dā**yoodoorahnt
emery board	en neglefil	ehn **nayler**feel
eye liner	en eye-liner	ehn ay-**layner**r
eye pencil	en øyenblyant	ehn oyernbl**ē**wahnt
eye shadow	en øyenskygge	ehn oyernsh**ew**gger
face flannel	en vaskeklut	ehn **vahss**kerkl**ē**wt
face pack	en ansiktsmaske	ehn **ahn**ssiktsmahssker
face powder	et pudder til ansiktet	eht **pewd**derr til **ahn**ssikter
foot cream	en fotkrem	ehn **fōōt**krāym
hand cream	en håndkrem	ehn **hon**krāym
lipsalve	en leppepomade	ehn **lehp**perpoomaader
lipstick	en leppestift	ehn **lehp**persstift
lipstick brush	en leppestift-pensel	ehn **lehp**persstift-pehnsserl
make-up bag	en sminkeveske	ehn **sminker**vehssker
make-up remover pads	vattdotter til å fjerne make-up	**vaht**dotterr til aw fy**ā**'ner mayk-ewp
mascara	maskara	ehn mahss**kaar**ah
nail brush	en neglebørste	ehn **nayler**burshter
nail clippers	en negleklipper	ehn **nayler**klipperr
nail file	en neglefil	ehn **nayler**feel
nail polish	en neglelakk	ehn **nayler**lahk
nail-polish remover	en neglelakkfjerner	ehn **nayler**lahk-fy**ā**'nerr
nail scissors	en neglesaks	ehn **nayler**ssahks
nail strengthener	et styrkemiddel til neglene	eht **stewr**kermidderl til **nayler**ner
paper handkerchiefs	en eske papir-lommetørklær	ehn **ehss**ker pahp**eer**-loommerturrkl**æ**r
perfume	en parfyme	ehn pahrf**ew**mer
powder puff	en pudderkvast	ehn **pewd**dehrkvahsst

rouge	en rouge	ehn rōōsh
safety pins	noen sikkerhetsnåler	nōōern sikkehrhāytsnawlerr
shaving brush	en barberkost	ehn bahrbāyrkoosst
shaving cream	en barberkrem	ehn bahrbāyrkrāym
shaving soap	en barbersåpe	ehn bahrbāyrssawper
soap	en såpe	ehn sawper
sun-tan cream/oil	en solkrem/-olje	ehn sōōl-krāym/-olyer
talcum powder	et talkum	eht tahlkewm
tissues	ansiktsservietter	ahnssiktssærvyehtterr
toilet paper	en rull toalettpapir	ehn rewl tooahlehtpahpeer
toilet water	et toalettvann	eht tooahlehtvahn
toothbrush	en tannbørste	ehn tahnburshter
toothpaste	en tannpasta	ehn tahnpahsstah
towel	et håndkle	eht honklāy
tweezers	en pinsett	ehn pinsseht
washcloth	en vaskeklut	ehn vahsskerklewt

For your hair

bobby pins	noen hårnåler	nōōern hawrnawlerr
comb	en kam	ehn kahm
curlers	noen ruller	nōōern rewllerr
dye	et hårfargingsmiddel	eht hawrfahrgingssmidderl
grips	noen klips	nōōern klips
hair brush	en hårbørste	ehn hawrburshter
hair colouring	et hårfargingsmiddel	eht hawrfahrgingssmidderl
hair net	et hårnett	eht hawrneht
hair oil	en hårolje	ehn hawrolyer
hair pins	noen hårspenner	nōōern hawrsspehnnerr
hair spray	en hårspray	ehn hawrspray
rollers	noen hårruller	nōōern hawr-rewllerr
setting lotion	et leggevann	eht lehggervahn

For the baby

baby cream	en babykrem	ehn bāybikrāym
baby food	babymat	bāybimaat
baby powder	et babypudder	eht bāybipewdderr
beaker (tumbler)	et krus	eht krēwss
bib	en smekke	ehn smehkker
dummy (pacifier)	en narresmokk	ehn nahrrersmook
nappies (diapers)	bleier	blayerr
nappy pins	noen bleie-sikker-hetsnåler	nōōern blayer-sikkerr-hāytsnawlerr
plastic pants	en plastbukse	ehn plahsstbookser

Clothing

If you want to buy something specific, prepare yourself in advance. Look at the list of clothing on page 117. Get some idea of the colour, material and size you want. They're all listed on the next few pages.

General

I'd like...	**Jeg vil gjerne ha...**	yay vil y**æ'**ner haa
I want...for a 10-year-old boy.	**Jeg vil gjerne ha... til en gutt på 10 år.**	yay vil y**æ'**ner haa... til ehn gewt paw 10 awr
I want something like this.	**Jeg skal ha noe liknende dette.**	yay skahl haa n**ōō**er liknehnder **deht**ter
How much is that per metre?	**Hva koster det for meteren?**	vah koss**terr** d**ā**y for m**ā**yterrern

1 centimetre	= 2/5 in.	1 inch = 2.54 cm.
1 metre	= 3 ft. 3 ³/₈ in.	1 foot = 30.5 cm.
10 metres	= 32 ft. 9 ³/₄ in.	1 yard = 0.91 m.

Colour

I want something in...	**Jeg vil gjerne ha noe i...**	yay vil y**æ'**ner haa n**ōō**er ee
I want something to match this.	**Jeg skal ha noe som passer til denne.**	yay skahl haa n**ōō**er som **pahs**serr til **dehn**ner
I don't like the colour.	**Jeg liker ikke fargen.**	yay **lee**kerr ikker **fahr**gern

ensfarget
(**ā**ynssfahrgert)

stripete
(**stree**perter)

prikkete
(**prik**kerter)

rutete
(r**ēw**terter)

mønstret
(**murns**strert)

beige	beige	bāysh
black	svart	svah't
blue	blå	blaw
brown	brun	brewn
cream	kremfarget	krāymfahrgert
crimson	høyrød	hoyrūr
emerald	smaragdgrønn	smahrahgd-grurn
fawn	lysebrun	lewsserbrewn
gold	gyllen	yewllern
green	grønn	grurn
grey	grå	graw
mauve	lilla	lillah
orange	oransje	oorahnsh
pink	lyserød	lewsser-rūr
purple	mørkerød	murrker-rūr
red	rød	rūr
scarlet	skarlagensrød	skahrlaagernssrūr
silver	sølvfarget	surlfahrgert
tan	brunaktig	brewnahkti
turquoise	turkis	tewrkeess
white	hvit	veet
yellow	gul	gewl

SHOPPING-GUIDE

Material

Do you have anything in...?	Har De noe i...?	haar dee nōōer ee
I want a cotton blouse.	Jeg vil gjerne ha en bomullsbluse.	yay vil yǣ'rner haa ehn boomewlssblewsser
Is it...?	Er det...?	ǣr dāy
a permanent crease	strykefritt	strēwkerfrit
hand-made	håndlaget	hawnlaagert
imported	importert	impoo'tāy't
made here	laget her	laagert hǣr
synthetic	syntetisk	sewntāytisk
tapered	innsvinget	inssvingert
wash-and-wear	strykefritt	strēwkerfrit
wrinkle-free	krøllfritt	krurlfrit
I want something...	Jeg vil ha noe...	yay vil haa nōōer
lighter/heavier	lettere/kraftigere	lehtterer/krahfteeerrer
Do you have any better quality?	Har De en bedre kvalitet?	haar dee ehn bāydrer kvahlitāyt

What's it made of?	Hva er den laget av?	vah ær dehn laaggert ahv

It may be made of...

cambric	batist	bahtisst
camel-hair	kamelhår	kahmaylhawr
chiffon	chiffon	shiffong
corduroy	kordfløyel	ko'dfloyerl
cotton	bomull	boomewl
crêpe	krepp	krehp
denim	denim / bomullstøy	dehnim / boomewlsstoy
felt	filt	filt
flannel	flanell	flahnehl
gabardine	gabardin	gahbahrdeen
lace	knipling	knipling
leather	lær	lær
linen	lin	leen
needlecord	tynnstripet kordfløyel	tewnstreepert ko'dfloyerl
nylon	nylon	newlon
pique	piké	pikay
poplin	poplin	popleen
rayon	rayon	rayon
satin	sateng	sahtehng
seersucker	stripet bomullsstoff	streepert boomewlsstof
serge	sterkt ullstoff	stærkt ewlstof
silk	silke	silker
suède	semsket skinn	sehmsskert shin
taffeta	taft	tahft
terrycloth	frotté	frottay
towelling	håndklestoff	hawnklaysstof
tulle	tyll	tewl
tweed	tweed	tveed
velvet	fløyel	floyerl
velour	velur	vehlewr
wool	ull	ewl
worsted	kamgarn	kahmgaarn

Size

My size is 38.	Jeg bruker størrelse 38.	yay brewker sturrerlsser 38
Could you measure me?	Kan De ta mål av meg?	kahn dee tah mawl ahv may
I don't know the Norwegian sizes.	Jeg kjenner ikke de norske størrelsene.	yay khehnnerr ikker dee noshker sturrerlsserner

In that case, look at the charts opposite.

This is your size

Ladies

Dresses/Suits					
American	10	12	14	16	18	20
British	32	34	36	38	40	42
Continental	38	40	42	44	46	48

Stockings							Shoes			
American } British }	8	8½	9	9½	10	10½	6 4½	7 5½	8 6½	9 7½
Continental	0	1	2	3	4	5	37	38	40	41

Gentlemen

Suits/Overcoats							Shirts			
American } British }	36	38	40	42	44	46	15	16	17	18
Continental	46	48	50	52	54	56	38	41	43	45

Shoes								
American } British }	5	6	7	8	8½	9	9½	10	11
Continental	38	39	41	42	43	43	44	44	45

In Europe sizes vary somewhat from country to country, so the above must be taken as an approximate guide.

A good fit?

Can I try it on?	**Kan jeg prøve det på?**	kahn yay prūrver dāy paw
Where's the fitting room?	**Hvor er prøve-rommet?**	voor ær prūrver-roommer
Is there a mirror?	**Er det et speil et sted?**	ær dāy eht spayl eht stāy
Does it fit?	**Passer det?**	pahsserr dāy

FOR NUMBERS, see page 175

SHOPPING-GUIDE

It fits very well.	Det passer veldig bra.	dāy pahsserr vehldi braa
It doesn't fit.	Det passer ikke.	dāy pahsserr ikker
It's too...	Det er for...	dāy ǣr for
short/long	kort/langt	ko't/lahngt
tight/loose	trangt/vidt	trahngt/vit
How long will it take to alter?	Hvor lang tid vil det ta å forandre det?	voor lahng teed vil dāy taa aw forahndrer dāy

Shoes

I'd like a pair of...	Jeg vil gjerne ha et par...	yay vil yǣ'ner haa eht paar
shoes/sandals	sko/sandaler	skōō/sahndaalerr
boots/slippers	støvler/tøfler	sturvlerr/turflerr
These are too...	Disse er for...	disser ǣr for
narrow/wide	trange/vide	trahnger/veeder
large/small	store/små	stōōrer/smaw
They pinch my toes.	De klemmer over tærne.	dee klehmmerr awverr tǣ'ner
Do you have a larger size?	Har De et større nummer?	haar dee eht sturrer noommerr
I want a smaller size.	Jeg vil gjerne ha et nummer mindre.	yay vil yǣ'ner haa eht noommerr mindrer
Do you have the same in...?	Har De de samme i...?	haar dee dee sahmmer ee
brown/beige	brunt/beige	brewnt/bāysh
black/white	svart/hvitt	svah't/vit
I'd like some shoe polish/shoe laces.	Jeg vil gjerne ha skokrem/skolisser.	yay vil yǣ'ner haa skōōkraym/skōōlisserr
Can you repair these shoes?	Kan De reparere disse skoene?	kahn dee rerpahrāyrer disser skōōerner
I want new soles and heels.	Jeg vil gjerne ha nye såler og hæler.	yay vil yǣ'ner haa nēwer sawlerr o hāylerr
When will they be ready?	Når er de ferdige?	nawr ǣr dee fǣr'deeer
I'd like a shine.	Jeg vil gjerne ha skoene pusset.	yay vil yǣ'ner haa skōōehner pewssert

Clothes and Accessories

I'd like a/an/some...	Jeg vil gjerne ha...	yay vil yǣˈner haa
anorak	en anorakk	ehn anoorahk
bathing cap	en badehette	ehn baaderhehtter
bathing suit	en badedrakt	ehn baaderdrahkt
bath robe	en badekåpe	ehn baaderkawper
blouse	en bluse	ehn blewsser
bra	en brystholder	ehn brewssthollerr
braces	et par seler	eht paar sāylerr
briefs	et par korte under- bukser	eht paar koˈter ewnnerr- booksserr
cap	en lue	ehn lēwer
cardigan	en lett strikkejakke	ehn let strikkeryahkker
coat	en kåpe	ehn kawper
costume	en drakt	ehn drahkt
dress	en kjole	ehn khōōler
dressing gown	en morgenkjole	ehn mawernkhōōler
evening dress (ladies)	en aftenkjole	ehn ahfternkhōōler
fur coat	en skinnkåpe	ehn shinnkawper
galoshes	et par kalosjer	eht paar kahlosherr
garter belt	et strømpebelte	eht strurmperbehlter
girdle	en hofteholder	ehn hofterhollerr
gloves	et par hansker	eht paar hahnskerr
handkerchief	et lommetørkle	eht loommerturrkler
hat	en hatt	ehn haht
housecoat	en morgenkåpe	ehn mawernkawper
jacket	en jakke	ehn yahkker
jeans	et par ola-bukser	eht paar ōōlahbooksserr
jersey	en genser	ehn gehnsserr
jumper (Br.)	en tykk genser	ehn tewk gehnsserr
jumper (Am.)	en jumper	ehn jewmperr
lingerie	noe undertøy	nōōer ewnnertoy
nightdress	en nattkjole	ehn nahtkhōōler
overalls	en overall	ehn awvehrahl
overcoat	en ytterfrakk	ehn ewtterrfrahk
panties	panties	pæntiss
pants suit	en buksedress	ehn booksserdrehss
panty-girdle	en panty	ehn pænti
panty hose	en strømpebukse	ehn strurmperbooksser
pullover	en genser	ehn gehnsserr
pyjamas	en pyjamas	ehn pewshaamahss
raincoat	en regnfrakk	ehn raynfrahk
rubber boots	et par gummistøvler	eht paar gewmmissturvlerr
sandals	et par sandaler	eht paar sahndaalerr
scarf	et skjerf	eht shærf
shirt	en skjorte	ehn shooˈter

shoes	et par sko	eht paar sk$\overline{oo}$
shorts	en shorts	ehn shaw'ts
skirt	et skjørt	eht shur't
slip	en underkjole	ehn ewnnerrkh$\overline{oo}$ler
slippers	et par tøfler	eht paar turflerr
socks	et par sokker	eht paar sokkerr
stockings	et par strømper	eht paar strurmperr
suit (men's)	en dress	ehn drehss
suit (ladies')	en drakt	ehn drahkt
suspender belt	et strømpebelte	eht strurmperbehlter
suspenders	et par seler	eht paar s$\overline{ay}$lerr
sweater	en genser	ehn gehnsserr
sweatshirt	en bomullsgenser	ehn boomewlssgehnsserr
T-shirt	en T-skjorte	ehn t$\overline{ay}$-shoo'ter
tennis shoes	et par tennis-sko	eht paar tehnniss-sk$\overline{oo}$
tie	et slips	eht slips
tights	en strømpebukse	ehn strurmperbooksser
towel	et håndkle	eht hawnkl$\overline{ay}$
track suit	en treningsdrakt	ehn tr$\overline{ay}$ningssdrahkt
trousers	et par bukser	eht paar booksserr
twinset	et cardigan-sett	eht kaa'digahn-set
umbrella	en paraply	ehn pahrahpl$\overline{ew}$
underpants (men's)	et par herreunder-bukser	eht paar hærrerewnnerr-booksserr
undershirt	en undertrøye	ehn ewnnertroyer
vest (Am.)	en vest	ehn vehsst
vest (Br.)	en undertrøye	ehn ewnnertroyer
waistcoat	en vest	ehn vehsst

belt	belte	behlter
buckle	spenne	spehnner
button	knapp	knahp
collar	krave	kraaver
cuffs	mansjetter	mahnshehtterr
elastic	strikk	strik
hem	søm	surm
lapel	jakkeoppslag	yahkker-opslaag
lining	fôr	f$\overline{oo}$r
pocket	lomme	loommer
ribbon	bånd	bon
sleeve	erme	$\overline{ae}$rmer
zip (zipper)	glidelås	gleederlawss

Electrical appliances and accessories—Records

The voltage all over Norway is 220 v. A.C., 50 cycles.

I want a plug for this.	**Jeg vil gjerne ha et støpsel til denne.**	yay vil yǣ'ner haa eht sturpserl til dehnner
Do you have a battery for this...?	**Har De et batteri til denne...?**	haar dee eht bahtterree til dehnner
This is broken. Can your repair it?	**Denne er i stykker. Kan De reparere den?**	dehnner ǣr ee stewkkerr. kahn dee rehpahrāyrer dehn
When will it be ready?	**Når er den ferdig?**	nawr ǣr dehn fǣr'di
I'd like a/an/some...	**Jeg vil gjerne ha...**	yay vil yǣ'ner haa
adaptor	**en overgangs-kontakt**	ehn awverrgahngss-kontahkt
amplifier	**en forsterker**	ehn foshtǣrkerr
battery	**et batteri**	eht bahtterree
blender	**en mix master**	ehn miksmaasterr
bulb	**en lyspære**	ehn lēwsspærer
clock	**en klokke**	ehn klokker
wall clock	**et veggur**	eht vehggēwr
extension cord	**en skjøteledning**	ehn shūrterlehdning
food mixer	**en håndmikser**	ehn hawnmikserr
hair dryer	**en hårtørrer**	ehn haw'turrerr
iron	**et strykejern**	eht strēwkeryǣ'n
travelling-iron	**et reisestrykejern**	eht raysserstrēwker-yǣ'n
kettle	**en kjele**	ehn khāyler
percolator	**en kaffetrakter**	ehn kahffertrahkterr
plug	**et støpsel**	eht sturpserl
radio	**en radio**	ehn raadio
car radio	**en bilradio**	ehn beelraadio
portable radio	**en reiseradio**	ehn raysser-raadio
razor	**en barbermaskin**	ehn bahrbāyrmahsheen
record player	**en platespiller**	ehn plaaterspillerr
portable record-player	**en reise-grammo-fon**	ehn raysser-grahmmoo-fōōn
speakers	**noen høyttalere**	nōōern hoytaalerer
tape recorder	**en båndopptaker**	ehn bawnoptaakerr
cassette tape-recorder	**en kassett-bånd-opptaker**	ehn kahseht-bawn-optaakerr
portable tape-recorder	**en reisebånd-opptaker**	ehn raysser-bawnop-taakerr

SHOPPING-GUIDE

television	et TV-apparat	eht tāyvāy-ahppahraat
colour television	farge-TV	fahrger-tāyvāy
portable television	reise-TV	raysser-tāyvāy
toaster	en brødrister	ehn brūr-rissterr
transformer	en transformator	ehn trahnsfoormaatoor

Record shop

Do you have any records by...?	Har De noen plater av...?	haar dee nōōern plaaterr ahv
Do you have...'s latest album?	Har De den siste platen av...?	haar dee dehn sisster plaatern ahv
Can I listen to this record?	Kan jeg få høre på denne platen?	kahn yay faw hūrrer paw dehnner plaatern
I'd like a cassette.	Jeg vil gjerne ha en kassett.	yay vil yǣ'ner haa ehn kahsseht
I want a new needle.	Jeg vil gjerne ha en ny stift.	yay vil yǣ'ner haa ehn new stift

33/45 rpm	33/45 omdreininger pr. minutt	trehttitrāy/fur'tifehm omdrayningerr pær minewt
mono/stereo	mono/stereo	mōōnoo/stāyrio

chamber music	kammermusikk	kahmmerrmewssik
classical music	klassisk musikk	klahssisk mewssik
folk music	folkemusikk	folkermewssik
instrumental music	instrumentalmusikk	instrewmehntaalmewssik
jazz	jazz	yahss
light music	lett musikk	leht mewssik
orchestral music	orkestermusikk	orkehssterr-mewssik
pop music	popmusikk	popmewssik

Hairdressing

Barber's

I don't speak much Norwegian.	Jeg snakker ikke mye norsk.	yay snahkkerr ikker mēwer noshk
I'm in a hurry.	Jeg har liten tid.	yay haar leetern teed
I want a haircut, please.	Jeg vil gjerne få klippet håret.	yay vil yǣ'ner faw klippert hawrer
I'd like a shave.	Jeg vil gjerne barberes.	yay vil yǣ'ner bahrbāyrerss
Don't cut it too short.	Ikke klipp det for kort, er De snill.	ikker klip dāy for ko't ǣr dee snil
Scissors only, please.	Bare saks, vær så snill.	baarer sahks, vǣr saw snil
A razor cut, please.	Jeg vil gjerne ha fjærklipp.	yay vil yǣ'ner haa fyǣrklip
Don't use the clippers.	Ikke bruk klipperen.	ikker brēwk klipperrern
Just a trim, please.	Jeg vil bare ha det stusset.	yay vil baarer haa dāy stewssert
That's enough off.	Det er nok.	dāy ǣr nok
A little more off the...	Litt mere av..., er De snill.	lit māyrer ahv...ǣr dee snil
back	bak	baak
neck	i nakken	ee nahkkern
sides	på sidene	paw seederner
top	oppå	oppaw
Please don't use any oil/cream.	Jeg vil ikke ha olje/krem.	yay vil ikker haa olyer/krāym
Would you please trim my...?	Vil De være så snill å stusse...?	vil dee vǣrer saw snil aw stewsser
beard	skjegget mitt	shehgger mit
moustache	barten min	bah'tern min
sideboards (sideburns)	kinnskjegget mitt	khinshehgger mit
Thank you. That's fine.	Tusen takk. Det er bra.	tēwssern tahk. dāy ǣr braa
How much do I owe you?	Hva koster det?	vah kossterr dāy
This is for you.	Dette er til Dem.	dehtter ǣr til dehm

SHOPPING GUIDE

Ladies' hairdresser's—Beauty salon

Is there a hairdresser's in the hotel?	**Finnes det en dame-frisørsalong på hotellet?**	finners dāy ehn daamer-frissūūrsahlong paw hootehller
Can I make an appointment for sometime on Thursday?	**Kan jeg få bestilt en time til torsdag?**	kahn yay faw berstilt ehn teemer til toshdaag
I'd like it cut and shaped.	**Jeg vil gjerne ha klipp, vask og legg.**	yay vil yǣ'ner haa klip vahssk o lehg

with a fringe (bangs)	**med lugg**	māy lewg
page-boy style	**pasjehår**	paasherhawr
a razor cut	**fjærklippet**	fyǣrklippert
a re-style	**noe nytt**	nōōer newt
with ringlets	**med lokker**	māy lokkerr
with waves	**med bølger**	māy burlggerr
in a bun	**i topp**	ee top

I want a...	**Jeg vil gjerne ha...**	yay vil yǣ'ner haa
bleach	**bleking**	blāyking
colour rinse	**fargeskylling**	fahrgershewlling
dye	**håret farget**	hawrer fahrgert
permanent wave	**permanent**	pærmahnehnt
shampoo and set	**vask og legg**	vahsk o lehg
tint	**håret tonet**	hawrer tōōnert
touch up	**gredd opp**	grehd op

I want...	**Jeg vil gjerne ha...**	yay vil yǣ'ner haa
the same colour	**samme farge**	sahmmer fahrger
a darker colour	**en mørkere farge**	ehn murrkehrer fahrger
a lighter colour	**en lysere farge**	ehn lēwssehrer fahrger
auburn/blond/brunette	**kastanje/blond/brunette**	kahsstahnyer/blond/brewnehtter

Do you have a colour chart?	**Har De et fargekart?**	haar dee eht fahrgerkahrt
I don't want any hairspray.	**Jeg vil ikke ha hårspray.**	yay vil ikker haa hawrspräy
I want a...	**Jeg vil gjerne ha...**	yay vil yǣ'ner haa
manicure/pedicure	**manikyr/pedikyr**	mahnikēwr/pehdikēwr
face-pack	**ansiktsmaske**	ahnssiktssmahssker

Jeweller's—Watchmaker's

Jewellery shops and watchmakers' are separate establishments in Norway. In the jeweller's, notice the colourful enamel work for which Norwegian craftsmen are famous.

Can you repair this watch?	Kan De reparere denne klokken?	kahn dee rehpahrāyrer dehnner klokkern
The...is broken.	...er gått i stykker.	...ār got ee stewkkerr
glass/spring strap winder	glasset/fjæren remmen opptrekkskruen	glahsser/fyā̄rern rehmmern optrehksskrēwern
When will it be ready?	Når vil den være ferdig?	nawr vil dehn vā̄rer fā̄'di
Could I please see that?	Kan jeg få se på den?	kahn yay faw sāy paw dehn
I'm just looking around.	Jeg bare ser meg litt rundt.	yay baarer sāyr may lit rewnt
I'd like a cheap watch.	Jeg vil gjerne ha en billig klokke.	yay vil yā̄'ner haa ehn billi klokker
I want a small gift.	Jeg skal ha en liten presang.	yay skahl haa ehn leetern prehssang
I don't want anything too expensive.	Jeg vil ikke ha noe som er for dyrt.	yay vil ikker haa nō̄er som ār for dew't
I want something...	Jeg vil ha noe...	yay vil haa nō̄er
better/cheaper/ simpler	bedre/billigere/ enklere	bāydrer/billeeehrer/ ehnklehrer
Do you have anything in gold?	Har De noe i gull?	haar dee nō̄er ee gewl
How many carats is this?	Hvor mange karat er det?	voor mahnger kahraat ār dāy
Is this real silver?	Er det ekte sølv?	ār dāy ehkter surl
Can you engrave my initials on it?	Vil De gravere mine initialer på det?	vil dee grahvāyrer meener inisseeaalerr paw dāy

When you go to a jeweller's, you've probably got some idea of what you want beforehand. Use the following lists to find out what the article is called and what it's made of.

124

What is it?

I'd like a/an/some...	Jeg vil gjerne ha...	yay vil **yɜ̄**'ner haa
bangle	en armring	ehn **ahrm**ring
beads	perler	**pɜ̄**'lerr
bracelet	et armbånd	eht **ahrm**bon
charm bracelet	et charms-armbånd	eht **sharmss**-ahrmbon
brooch	en brosje	ehn **bros**her
chain	et kjede	eht **khāy**der
charm	et anheng	eht **ahn**hehng
cigarette case	et sigarett-etui	eht siggah**reht**-ehtewee
cigarette lighter	en lighter	ehn **lay**terr
clip	noen klips	**nōō**ern klips
clock	en klokke	ehn **klok**ker
alarm clock	en vekkerklokke	ehn **vehk**kerrklokker
travelling clock	en reisevekker-klokke	ehn **rays**servehkkerr-klokker
cross	et kors	eht kosh
cuff-links	noen mansjett-knapper	**nōō**ern mahn**sheht**-knahpperr
cutlery	spisebestikk	**spees**serbersstik
earrings	noen øreringer	**nōō**ern **ūrr**erringerr
jewel box	et smykkeskrin	eht **smewk**kerskreen
manicure set	et manikyrsett	eht mahni**kewr**rsseht
mechanical pencil	en skrublyant	ehn **skrewb**lewawnt
necklace	et halsbånd	eht **hahls**sbon
pendant	et hengesmykke	eht **hehng**erssmewkker
pin	en nål	ehn nawl
powder compact	en pudderdåse	ehn **pewd**derrdawsser
propelling pencil	en skrublyant	ehn **skrewb**lewawnt
ring	en ring	ehn ring
engagement ring	en forlovelsesring	ehn for**lawv**erlssersssring
signet ring	en signetring	ehn sig**nāy**tring
wedding ring	en giftering	ehn **yif**terring
rosary	en rosenkrans	ehn **rōōs**sernkrahnss
silverware	noe sølvtøy	**nōō**er surltoy
snuff box	en snusdåse	ehn **snew**ssdawsser
strap	en rem	ehn rehm
tie clip	en slipsklemme	ehn **slips**klehmmer
tie pin	en slipsnål	ehn **slips**nawl
vanity case	et kosmetikkskrin	eht kooss**meht**iksskreen
watch	en klokke	ehn **klok**ker
calendar watch	en datoklokke	ehn **daa**tooklokker
pocket watch	et lommeur	eht **loom**merewr
wrist watch	et armbåndsur	eht ahrm**bonss**ewr
shock resistant	støtsikkert	**stūrt**ssikkerrt
waterproof	vanntett	**vahn**teht

SHOPPING-GUIDE

with a seconds hand	med sekundviser	maȳ sehkewnveesserr
watch band	en klokkerem	ehn klokkerrehm
expansion band	en ekspansjonsrem	ehn ekspahnshōōnss-rehm
leather band	en lærrem	ehn lǣrrehm

What's it made of?

alabaster	alabast	ahlahbahsst
amber	rav	raav
amethyst	ametyst	ahmertewsst
brass	messing	mehssing
bronze	bronse	bronsser
chromium	krom	kroom
copper	kopper	kopperr
coral	korall	koorahl
crystal	krystall	krewsstahl
cut glass	slepet glass	slaȳpert glahss
diamond	diamant	deeahmahnt
ebony	ibenholt	eebernholt
emerald	smaragd	smahrahgd
enamel	emalje	ehmahlyer
glass	glass	glahss
gold	gull	gewl
gold plate	gullplett	gewlpleht
ivory	elfenben	ehlfernbāȳn
jade	jade	yaader
marble	marmor	mahrmoor
onyx	onyks	ōōnewks
pearl	perle	pǣ'ler
pewter	tinn	tin
platinum	platina	plaatinah
ruby	rubin	rewbeen
sapphire	safir	sahfeer
silver	sølv	surl
silver plate	sølvplett	surlpleht
stainless steel	rustfritt stål	rewsstfrit stawl
topaz	topas	toopaass
turquoise	turkis	tewrkeess

Laundry—Dry cleaning

If your hotel doesn't have its own laundry or dry-cleaning service, ask the desk clerk:

English	Norwegian	Pronunciation
Where's the nearest laundry/dry-cleaner's?	Hvor er nærmeste vaskeri/renseri?	voor ær nærmehsster vahsskehree/rehnssehree
I want these clothes...	Jeg vil gjerne ha disse klærne...	yay vil yær'ner haa disser klær'ner
cleaned	renset	rehnssert
ironed	strøket	strūrkert
pressed	presset	prehssert
washed	vasket	vahsskert
When will it be ready?	Når er det ferdig?	nawr ær day fær'di
I need it...	Jeg trenger det...	yay trehngerr day
today	i dag	ee daag
tonight	i kveld	ee kvehl
tomorrow	i morgen	ee mawern
before Friday	før fredag	fūrr frāydaag
I want it as soon as possible.	Jeg vil gjerne ha det så fort som mulig.	yay vil yær'ner haa day saw foo't som mēwli
Can you...this?	Kan De...dette?	kahn dee...dehtter
mend	reparere	rehpahrāyrer
patch	lappe	lahpper
stitch	sy	sēw
Can you sew on this button?	Kan De sy i denne knappen?	kahn dee sēw ee dehnner knahppern
Can you get this stain out?	Kan De få vekk denne flekken?	kahn dee faw vehk dehnner flehkkern
Can this be invisibly mended?	Kan De kunststoppe dette?	kahn dee kewnsststopper dehtter
This isn't mine.	Denne er ikke min.	dehnner ær ikker meen
There's one piece missing.	Det mangler et plagg.	dāy mahnglerr eht plahg
There's a hole in this.	Det er et hull her.	dāy ær eht hewl hær
Is my laundry ready?	Er tøyet mitt ferdig?	ær toyer mit fær'di

Photography—Cameras

| I want an inexpensive camera. | **Jeg vil gjerne ha et rimelig fotografi-apparat.** | yay vil **yæ**'ner haa eht **ree**merli footoo-grahfee**ahp**pahraat |
| Show me the one in the window. | **Vil De vise meg det som er i vinduet?** | vil dee **vee**sser may **day** som **ær** ee vind**ew**er |

Film

Basic still and home movie exposure readings are given in English in the instructions with the roll.

Film sizes aren't always indicated the same way in Norway as in Great Britain and the United States.

$$110 = 13 \times 17$$
$$120 = 6 \times 6$$
$$126 = 26 \times 26$$
$$127 = 4 \times 4$$
$$135^* = 24 \times 36$$
$$620 = 6 \times 6$$

I'd like a...	**Jeg vil gjerne ha en...**	yay vil **yæ**'ner haa ehn
film for this camera	**film til dette appa-ratet**	film til **deh**tter ahppahra**at**er
colour film	**fargefilm**	**fahr**gerfilm
black-and-white film	**svart/hvitt-film**	**svah't/vit**-film
Polaroid film	**polaroidfilm**	poolahroo**eed**film
cartridge	**filmpatron**	**film**pahtroon
20/36 exposures	**20/36 bilder**	kh**ew**er/trehtti**ssehks** bilderr
this ASA/DIN number	**dette ASA/DIN nummer**	**deh**tter **aas**sah/deen **noom**merr
fast film	**hurtigfilm**	**hewr**tifilm
fine-grain film	**finkornet film**	feen**koo**'nert film
colour negatives	**fargenegativer**	fahrgernehgah**tee**verr
colour reversal	**fargereversering**	fahrger-rehvær**ssay**ring
colour slides	**fargeslides**	**fahr**ger-slayds

* 35-mm film

FOR NUMBERS, see page 175

artificial light type (indoor)	for kunstig belysning	for kewnssti behlewssning
daylight type (outdoor)	for dagslys	for dahgsslewss
8-mm film	8 mm film	otter-millimehterr film
single 8	single 8	singerl-otter
super 8	super 8	sewperr-otter
16-mm film	16 mm film	saysstern-millimehterr film

Processing

Does the price include processing?	Er fremkalling inkludert i prisen?	ær frehmkahlling inklewday't ee preessern
Will you develop and print this?	Kan De fremkalle og kopiere denne?	kahn dee frehmkahller o koopeeayrer dehnner
I want...prints of each negative.	Jeg vil ha... kopier av hvert negativ.	yay vil haa... koopeeerr ahv væ't naygahteev
with a glossy finish	med blank overflate	may blahnk awverrflaater
with a mat finish	med matt overflate	may maht awverrflaater
this size	denne størrelsen	dehnner sturrerlssern
Will you please enlarge this?	Vil De være så snill å forstørre dette?	vil dee værer saw snil aw foshturrer dehtter
When will it be ready?	Når er det ferdig?	nawr ær day fæ'di

Accessories

I want a/an/some...	Jeg vil ha...	yay vil haa
cable release	en kabelutløser	ehn kaaberl-ewtlursserr
camera case	en kamera-veske	ehn kaamehrah-vehssker
electronic flash	en elektronisk blitz	ehn ehlehktroonisk blits
filter	et filter	eht filterr
polarizing	polariseringsfilter	poolahrissayringssfilterr
red	rødt	rurt
ultra-violet	ultrafiolett	ewltrahfiooleht
yellow	gult	gewlt
flash bulbs	noen blitzpærer	nooern blitspærerr
flash cubes	noen blitzkuber	nooern blitskewberr
lens	en linse	ehn linsser
telephoto	telelinse	taylerlinsser
wide-angle	vidvinkel-linse	veedvinkerl-linsser
lens cap	en linsebeskytter	ehn linsserbershewtterr
tripod	et stativ	eht stahteev

SHOPPING-GUIDE

Broken

This camera doesn't work. Can you repair it?	Dette kameraet virker ikke. Kan De reparere det?	dehtter kaameraher veerkerr ikker. kahn dee rehpah-rayrer day
The film is jammed.	Filmen har satt seg fast.	filmern hahr saht say fahsst
The knob won't turn.	Fremtrekkeren går ikke rundt.	frehmtrehkkerrern gawr ikker rewnt
There's something wrong with the...	Det er noe galt med...	day ær nooer gaalt may
automatic lens	den automatiske linsen	dehn owtoomaatisker linssern
exposure counter	eksponeringstelleren	ehkspoonayringsstehl-lerrern
diaphragm	lysfilteret	lewssfilterrer
film feed	filmfremtrekket	filmfrehmtrehkker
flash contact	blitzkontakten	blitskoontahktern
lens	linsen	linssern
lightmeter	lysmåleren	lewssmawlerrern
rangefinder	søkeren	surkerrern
shutter	lukkeren	lookkerrern

Shooting

Do you mind if I take a few photographs?	Kan jeg få lov til å ta noen bilder?	kahn yay faw lawv til aw taa nooern bilderr
May I take a picture of you?	Kan jeg få ta et bilde av Dem?	kahn yay faw taa eht bilder ahv dehm
Please stand over there.	Vær så snill å stå der borte.	vær saw snil aw staw dær boo'ter
I'll send you a print.	Jeg skal sende Dem en kopi.	yay skahl sehnner dehm ehn koopee

And if you want to ask someone to take *your* picture:

Would you mind taking my/our picture? Look through here and press this button.	Kunne De tenke Dem å ta et bilde av meg/oss? De ser her og trykker ned denne knappen.	kewnner dee tehnker dehm aw taa eht bilder ahv may/oss. dee sayr hær o trewkkerr nay dehnner knahppern

Provisions

Here's a basic list of food and drink that you might want on a picnic or for the occasional meal at home:

I'd like a/an/some...	Jeg vil gjerne ha...	yay vil y**ǣ**'ner haa
apples	noen epler	n**ōō**ern **eh**plerr
bananas	noen bananer	n**ōō**ern bah**naa**nerr
biscuits (Br.)	en pakke kjeks	ehn **pahk**ker kheks
bread	et brød	eht br**ūū**
butter	litt smør	lit smurr
cakes	noen kaker	n**ōō**ern **kaa**kerr
candy	sukkertøy	**sook**kerrtoy
cheese	litt ost	lit oost
chocolate bar	en sjokoladeplate	ehn shookoo**laa**derplaater
coffee	litt kaffe	lit **kah**ffay
cold cuts	litt kaldt kjøtt	lit kahlt khurt
cookies	en pakke kjeks	ehn **pahk**ker khehks
cooking-fat	litt smult	lit smewlt
crackers	noen salte kjeks	n**ōō**ern **sahl**ter kheks
cream	litt fløte	lit **flur**ter
crisps	litt potetgull	lit poot**ayt**gewl
cucumber	en agurk	ehn ah**gewrk**
eggs	noen egg	n**ōō**ern ehg
flour	litt mel	lit m**ayl**
frankfurters	noen pølser	n**ōō**ern **purl**sserr
ham	litt skinke	lit **shin**ker
hamburger	noen hamburgere	n**ōō**ern **hahm**bewrgerrer
ice-cream	en is	ehn eess
lemonade	en brus	ehn br**ew**ss
lemons	noen sitroner	n**ōō**ern sitr**ōō**nerr
lettuce	et salathode	eht sahl**aat**h**ōō**der
liver sausage	en leverpølse	ehn **leh**verrpurlsser
luncheon meat	en boks lunch-meat	ehn boks **lurnsh**-meet
milk	melk	mehlk
mustard	litt sennep	lit **sehn**nerp
noodles	nudler	**newd**lerr
oranges	noen appelsiner	n**ōō**ern ahperl**sseen**err
pepper	pepper	**pehp**perr
pickles	pickles	**pik**kerlss
potato chips	pommes-frites	pom**frit**
potatoes	poteter	poot**ay**terr
rolls	noen rundstykker	n**ōō**ern **rewn**stewkkerr
salad	litt salat	lit sah**laat**
salt	salt	sahlt
sandwiches	noen smørbrød	n**ōō**ern **smurr**br**ūū**

sausages	noen pølser	nōōern purlsserr
sugar	sukker	sookkerr
sweets	sukkertøy	sookkerrtoy
tea	te	teh
tomatoes	noen tomater	nōōern toomaaterr

And don't forget...

aluminium foil	aluminiumsfolie	ahlewmeeneeewmss-fōōleeer
bottle opener	flaskeåpner	flahssskerawpnerr
corkscrew	korketrekker	korkertrehkerr
matches	fyrstikker	fewshtikkerr
paper napkins	papirservietter	pahpeersærvyehtterr
paper towelling	papirhåndkle	pahpeerhawnklāy
plastic bags	plastposer	plahsstpōōsserr
tin (can) opener	boksåpner	boksawpnerr
wax paper	matpapir	maatpahpeer

Weights and measures

1 kilogram or kilo (kg) = 1000 grams (g)

| 100 g = 3½ oz | ½ kg = 1 lb 1½ oz |
| 200 g = 7 oz | 1 kg = 2 lb 3 oz |

1 oz = 28.35 g
1 lb = 453.60 g

1 litre (l) = 0.88 imp. quarts = 1.06 U.S. quarts

| 1 imp. quart = 1.14 l | 1 U.S. quart = 0.95 l |
| 1 imp. gallon = 4.55 l | 1 U.S. gallon = 3.8 l |

---

box	eske	ehssker
can	hermetikkboks	hærmehtikboks
carton	kartong	kahrtong
crate	kasse	kahsser
jar	krukke	krookker
packet	pakke	pahkker
tin	hermetikkboks	hærmehtikboks
tube	tube	tēwber

132

Souvenirs—Antiquities

The most likely Norwegian souvenirs to look for are products of home craftsmen.

We've already mentioned the colourful enamel work on sale at the jeweller's. Another good idea is knitwear, especially the *Selbu* designs used for sweaters, mittens, stockings, etc. The cottage industries also produce beautiful dolls in native costumes (*bunad*—**bēw**nahd).

Modern pottery and glass, wrought-iron and pewter articles are also in demand for souvenirs, especially the hand-made items of distinctive design.

In the north especially you can find souvenirs made of reindeer skin—as well as reindeer horns themselves.

Norwegian antiquities may not be exported. When in doubt the seller must obtain permission from the Norwegian Folk Museum.

I'd like a/an/some...	Jeg vil gjerne ha...	yay vil yæ'ner haa
bowl	en bolle	ehn boller
copper- and enamelware	noe i kopper og emalje	nōōer ee kopperr o ehmahlyer
gloves	et par hansker	eht paar hahnskerr
handcarved figure	en håndskåret figur	ehn honskawrert figg**ēw**r
horn souvenir	en suvenir av horn	ehn sewvehneer ahv hōōrn
mittens	et par votter	eht paar votterr
purse	en pung	ehn poong
reindeer skin	et reinsdyrskinn	eht raynss**dēw**rshin
reindeer-skin shoes	et par sko av reinsdyrskinn	eht paar skōō ahv raynss**dēw**rshin
reindeer-skin slippers	et par tøfler av reinsdyrskinn	eht paar turflerr ahv raynss**dēw**rshin
sealskin	et selskinn	eht s**ā**ylshin
silver	noe i sølv	nōōer ee surl
sweater	en kofte	ehn kofter
troll	et troll	eht trol
wood carving	en treskjæring	ehn tr**āy**sh**ǣ**ring

Tobacconist's

In Norway the popular makes of cigarettes have curiously foreign-sounding names—Long Fellow, Cooly, Teddy, South State. They're locally manufactured but quite expensive. Foreign cigarettes are heavily taxed as well, and therefore even more expensive.

I'd like a/an/some...	Jeg vil gjerne ha...	yay vil yær'ner haa
box of cigars	en eske sigarer	ehn ehssker siggaarerr
chewing tobacco	en eske skråtobakk	ehn ehssker skrawtoobahk
cigar	en sigar	ehn siggaar
cigarette case	et sigarettetui	eht siggahrehttehtewee
cigarette holder	et sigarettmunn-stykke	eht siggahrehtt-mewnsstewkker
cigarette lighter	en lighter	ehn layterr
flints	noen flintsteiner	nooern flintstaynerr
lighter fluid	lighter-bensin	layterr-behnsseen
lighter gas	lighter-gass	layterr-gahss
refill for a lighter	refill til en lighter	rerfill til ehn layterr
matches	en eske fyrstikker	ehn ehssker fewshtikkerr
packet of cigarettes	en pakke sigaretter	ehn pahkker siggahrehtterr
pipe	en pipe	ehn peeper
pipe cleaners	noen piperensere	nooern peeper-rehnsserrer
pipe rack	et pipestativ	eht peeperstahteev
pipe tobacco	noe pipetobakk	nooer peepertoobahk
pipe tool	en piperenser av metall	ehn peeperrehnsserr ahv mehtahl
snuff	en pakke snus	ehn pahkker snewss
tobacco pouch	en tobakkspung	ehn toobahkspoong
wick	en veke	ehn vayker

Do you have any...?	Har De noen...?	haar dee nooern
American cigarettes	amerikanske sigaretter	ahmehrikaansker siggahrehtterr
English cigarettes	engelske sigaretter	ehngerlsker siggahrehtterr
I'll take two packets.	Jeg tar to pakker.	yay taar too pahkkerr
I'd like a carton.	Jeg vil gjerne ha en kartong.	yay vil yær'ner haa ehn kah'tong

filter-tipped	filtersigaretter	filterr-siggahrehtterr
king-size	king size	king sayss
without filter	uten filter	ewtern filterr

Your money: banks—currency

At larger banks there's sure to be someone who speaks English. In most tourist centres you'll find small currency-exchange offices (vekslekontor—**vehks**lerkoontōōr), especially during the summer season. The exchange rates shouldn't vary much between them. Remember to take your passport with you, since you may need it.

Travellers' cheques and credit cards are widely accepted in tourist-oriented shops, hotels, restaurants etc. However, if you're exploring the countryside off the beaten track you mustn't expect every little village store to be acquainted with them, or with foreign currency. The same applies to garages and service stations.

Opening hours

Banks are open from 8.15 a.m. to 3/3.30 p.m., Monday to Friday. In the countryside the local banks normally work shorter hours. At Oslo Airport the exchange office operates from 7 a.m. till 10/11 p.m. every day.

Monetary unit

The basic unit of the Norwegian monetary system is the crown (krone—**krōō**ner) which is divided into 100 øre (**ūr**rer). The Norwegian abbreviation for crown is kr.

There are coins of 5, 10, 25 and 50 øre and of 1 and 5 crowns, and banknotes (sedler—**sehd**lerr) of 10, 50, 100, 500 and 1000 crowns.

Before going

| Where's the nearest bank/currency-exchange office? | Hvor er nærmeste bank/vekslekontor? | voor ær nærmehsster bahnk/**vehks**lerkoontōōr |

| Where can I cash a traveller's cheque? | Hvor kan jeg løse inn en reisesjekk? | voor kahn yay lūrsser in ehn rayssershehk |
| Where's the Kredittkassen? | Hvor er Kredittkassen? | voor ǣr krehdit-kahssern |

Inside

I want to change some dollars/pounds.	Jeg vil gjerne veksle noen dollar/pund.	yay vil yǣ'ner vehksler nōōern dollahr/pewn
What's the exchange rate?	Hva er kursen?	vah ǣr kēwshern
What rate of commission do you charge?	Hva tar De i kommisjon?	vah taar dee ee koomishōōn
Can you cash a personal cheque?	Kan De løse inn en personlig sjekk?	kahn dee lūrsser in ehn pæshōōnli shehk
How long will it take to clear?	Hvor lang tid tar det å klarere den?	voor lahng teed taar dāy aw klahrāyrer dehn
Can you wire my bank in...?	Kan De telegrafere til banken min i...?	kahn dee tehlehgrahfāyrer til bahnkern meen ee
I have...	Jeg har...	yay haar
a letter of credit	et akkreditiv	eht ahkrehditeev
an introduction from...	et introduksjonsbrev fra...	eht introodewkshōōnss-brāyv fraa
a credit card	et kredittkort	eht krehditko't
I'm expecting some money from Chicago. Has it arrived yet?	Jeg venter penger fra Chicago. Har de kommet?	yay vehnterr pehngerr frah shikaagōō. haar dee kommert
Please give me... notes (bills) and some small change.	Vil De være vennlig å gi meg... sedler og litt småpenger.	vil dee vǣrer vehnli aw yee may...sehdlerr o lit smawpehngerr
Give me...large notes and the rest in small notes.	Gi meg...i store sedler og resten i små sedler.	yee may...ee stōōrer sehdlerr o rehsstern ee smaw sehdlerr
Could you please check that again?	Kunne De være så vennlig å sjekke dette igjen?	kewnner dee vǣrer saw vehnli aw shehkker dehtter eeyehn

136

Depositing

I want to credit this to my account.	**Jeg vil gjerne sette dette inn på min konto.**	yay vil **yø̄'**ner **seht**ter **deht**ter in paw meen **kon**too
I want to credit this to Mr...'s account.	**Jeg vil gjerne at dette skal krediteres kontoen til herr...**	yay vil **yø̄'**ner aht **deht**ter skahl krehdit**āy**rerss **kon**toern til hærr
Where should I sign?	**Hvor skal jeg signere?**	voor skahl yay sigg**nāy**rer

Currency converter

In a world of fluctuating exchange rates, we can offer no more than this do-it-yourself chart. You can get a card showing current exchange rates from banks, travel agents and tourist offices. Why not fill in this chart, too, for handy reference?

Norway	£	$
10 øre		
50 øre		
1 krone		
10 kroner		
50 kroner		
100 kroner		
500 kroner		
1000 kroner		
5000 kroner		

FOR NUMBERS, see page 175

At the post-office

Norwegian letter-boxes are red and marked with the word *Post*. Stamps can be purchased at post-offices, kiosks, and stationers'; in the country most shops that sell picture postcards sell stamps.

Business hours at post-offices are generally from 8 a.m. till 5.30 p.m. (till 4.30 p.m. in summer), Monday to Friday, and 9 a.m. till 1 p.m., Saturday.

Where's the (nearest) post-office?	**Hvor er (nærmeste) posthus?**	voor **ær** (**nær**mehsster) poss**thew**ss
Can you tell me how to get to the post-office?	**Kan De fortelle meg hvordan jeg kommer til posthuset?**	kahn dee fo'**teh**ller may voo'dahn yay **kom**merr til poss**thew**sser
What time does the post-office open/close?	**Når åpner/stenger posthuset?**	nawr **awp**nerr/**stehng**err poss**thew**sser
What window do I go to for stamps?	**I hvilken luke får jeg frimerker?**	ee vilkern **few**ker fawr yay **free**mærkerr
At which counter can I cash an international money order?	**I hvilken luke kan jeg heve en internasjonal postanvisning?**	ee vilkern **few**ker kahn yay **hay**ver ehn interr-nahsh**oo**naal posstahn-veessning
I want some stamps, please.	**Jeg vil gjerne ha noen frimerker.**	yay vil **yæ**'ner haa **noo**ern **free**mærkerr
A stamp for this letter/postcard, please.	**Et frimerke til dette brevet/kortet.**	eht **free**mærker til **deh**tter **bray**vert/**ko**'tert
What's the postage for a letter to England?	**Hva koster et brev til England?**	vah **koss**terr eht **bray**v til **ehng**lahn
What's the postage for a postcard to the U.S.A.?	**Hva koster et post-kort til USA?**	vah **koss**terr eht posst-**ko**'t til ewehss**saa**
I want to send this parcel.	**Jeg vil gjerne sende denne pakken.**	yay vil **yæ**'ner **sehn**ner **dehn**ner **pahk**kern

Do I need to fill in a customs declaration?	Må jeg fylle ut en tolldeklarasjon?	maw yay fewller ewt ehn toldehklahrahshōōn
Where's the mail-box?	Hvor er post-kassen?	voor ær posstkahssern
I want to send this by...	Jeg vil gjerne sende dette med...	yay vil yæ'ner sehnner dehtter māy
airmail	luftpost	lewftposst
express (special delivery)	ekspress	eksprehss
registered mail	rekommandert	rehkoommahndāyrt
surface mail	ikke luftpost	ikker lewftposst
Where's the poste restante (general delivery)?	Hvor er poste restanteskranken?	voor ær posster rehstahn-terskrahnkern
Is there any mail for me? My name is...	Er det noe post til meg? Mitt navn er...	ær dāy nōōer posst til may. mit nahvn ær
Here's my passport.	Her er passet mitt.	hāēr ær pahsser mit

FRIMERKER	STAMPS
PAKKER	PARCELS
POSTANVISNINGER	MONEY ORDERS

Telegrams

Where's the (nearest) telegraph office?	Hvor er (nærmeste) telegrafkontor?	voor ær (nærmehsster) tehlehgraafkoontōōr
I want to send a telegram. May I please have a form?	Jeg vil gjerne sende et telegram. Kan jeg få en blankett?	yay vil yæ'ner sehnner eht tehlehgrahm. kahn yay faw ehn blahnkeht
How much is it per word?	Hva koster det pr. ord?	vah kossterr dāy pær ōōr
I'd like to reverse the charges.	Jeg vil gjerne at mottakeren betaler.	yay vil yæ'ner aht mōōttaakerrern bertaalerr
I'd like to send a night letter.	Jeg vil gjerne sende et brevtelegram.	yay vil yæ'ner sehnner eht brāyvtehlehgrahm

Telephoning

To make a local call first insert a 1-crown coin. You can dial directly to most places in Europe with the correct *forvalgnummer* (dialling prefix or area code).

General

Where's the telephone?	**Hvor er telefonen?**	voor **ær** tehlehf**oo**nern
Where's there a public telephone?	**Hvor finnes en offentlig telefon?**	voor **finn**ers en **off**erntli tehlehf**oo**n
May I use your phone?	**Kan jeg få låne telefonen Deres?**	kahn yay faw **law**ner tehlehf**oo**nern **day**rerss
Do you have a telephone directory for Oslo?	**Har De en telefonkatalog for Oslo?**	haar dee ehn tehlehf**oo**n-kahtahlawg for **ooss**loo
Can you help me get this number?	**Kan De hjelpe meg med å få dette nummeret?**	kahn dee **yehl**per may m**ay** aw faw **deht**ter **noom**merrer
Do you have change for the telephone?	**Har De vekslepenger til telefonen?**	haar dee **vehks**lerpehngerr til tehlehf**oo**nern

Operator

Do you speak English?	**Snakker De engelsk?**	**snahk**kerr dee **ehng**erlsk
Good morning, I want Bergen 12 34 56.	**God morgen, jeg vil gjerne ha Bergen 12 34 56.**	goo **maw**ern yay vil **yæ'**ner haa **bær**gern 12 34 56

Note: Numbers are given in pairs.

Can I dial direct?	**Kan jeg slå direkte?**	kahn yay slaw di**rehk**ter
I want to place a personal (person-to-person) call.	**Jeg vil gjerne ha en personlig samtale.**	yay vil **yæ'**ner haa ehn pæsh**oo**nli **sahm**taaler
I want to reverse the charges.	**Jeg vil gjerne at mottakeren betaler.**	yay vil **yæ'**ner aht **moot**-taakerrern ber**taa**lerr
Will you tell me the cost of the call afterwards?	**Vil De vennligst gi meg prisen på samtalen etter på?**	vil dee **vehn**ligst yee may **preess**ern paw **sahm**taalern **eht**terrpaw

FOR NUMBERS, see page 175

Speaking

Hello. This is... speaking.	**Hallo. Dette er...**	hahloo **deht**ter ær
I want to speak to...	**Jeg vil gjerne snakke med...**	yay vil yæ'ner **snahk**ker may
Would you put me through to...?	**Kunne De sette meg over til...?**	**kew**nner dee **seht**ter may awverr til
I want extension...	**Jeg vil gjerne ha linje...**	yay vil yæ'ner haa **lin**yer
Is that...?	**Er det...?**	ær day

Bad luck

Would you please try again later?	**Kunne De være så vennlig å prøve om igjen senere?**	**kew**nner dee **væ**rer saw **vehn**nli aw **pru**rver om eeyehn **say**nerrer
Operator, you gave me the wrong number.	**De ga meg et galt nummer.**	dee gaa may eht gaalt **noom**mer
Operator, we were cut off.	**Vi ble avbrutt.**	vee blay **aav**brewt

Telephone alphabet

A	**Anna**	ahnnah	O	**Olivia**	ooleeveeah
B	**Bernhard**	bæ'nhahrd	P	**Petter**	pehtterr
C	**Cæsar**	sayssahr	Q	**Quintus**	kvintewss
D	**David**	daavid	R	**Rikard**	rikahrd
E	**Edith**	aydit	S	**Sigrid**	sigree
F	**Fredrik**	frehdrik	T	**Teodor**	tayoodoor
G	**Gustav**	gewsstahv	U	**Ulrik**	ewlrik
H	**Harald**	hahrahl	V	**enkelt-V**	ehnkerlt-vay
I	**Ivar**	eevahr	W	**dobbelt-V**	dobberlt-vay
J	**Johan**	yohahn	X	**Xerxes**	ksærksserss
K	**Karin**	kaareen	Y	**Yngling**	ewngling
L	**Ludvig**	lewdvik	Z	**Zakarias**	sahkahreeahss
M	**Martin**	mah'tin	Æ	**Ærlig**	ærlee
N	**Nils**	nilss	Ø	**Ørn**	urrn
			Å	**Åse**	awsser

The connection was bad.	**Forbindelsen var dårlig.**	forbinnerlssern vaar **daw'li**
Would you please try the number again?	**Kunne De prøve nummeret om igjen?**	kewnner dee **pruūr**ver noommerrer om eeyehn

Not there

When will he/she be back?	**Når kommer han/ hun tilbake?**	nawr **kom**merr hahn/huhn tilbaaker
Will you tell him/her I called? My name's...	**Kan De si at jeg har ringt? Mitt navn er...**	kahn dee see aht yay haar ringt. mit nahvn **æ**r
Would you ask him/ her to call me?	**Kan De be ham/ henne å ringe meg?**	kahn dee **bay** hahm/ hehnner aw **ring**er may
Would you please take a message?	**Kunne De være så snill å ta imot en beskjed?**	kewnner dee **væ**rer saw snil aw taa eem**ōō**t ehn ber**shay**

Charges

What was the cost of that call?	**Hva kostet samtalen?**	vah **koss**tert **sahm**taalern
I want to pay for the call.	**Jeg vil gjerne betale for samtalen.**	yay vil **yæ**r'ner ber**taa**ler for **sahm**taalern

---

Det er telefon til Dem.	There's a telephone call for you.
Hvilket nummer ringer De?	What number are you calling?
Det er opptatt.	The line's engaged.
Det svarer ikke.	There's no answer.
De har fått galt nummer.	You've got the wrong number.
Telefonen er i ustand.	The phone is out of order.
Han/Hun er ute for øyeblikket.	He's/She's out at the moment.
Skal jeg prøve igjen senere?	Shall I try again later?

The car

This section is entirely devoted to motoring. It's been divided into three parts:

Part A (pages 142-145) contains the phrases that you'll need at the filling station and when asking the way.

Part B (pages 146-149) contains general advice on motoring in Norway, hints and regulations.

Part C (pages 150-159) is concerned with the practical details of breakdown and accidents. It includes a list of car parts and of the things that may go wrong with them. All you have to do is to show the list to the mechanic and get him to point to the repairs and items required.

Part A

Filling stations

Most filling stations don't handle major repairs, but apart from providing you with fuel they may be helpful in solving all kinds of minor problems.

Where's the nearest filling station?	Hvor er nærmeste bensinstasjon?	voor ær nærmehsster behnsseenstahshōōn
I want...litres of petrol (gas), please.	Jeg vil gjerne ha ...liter bensin.	yay vil yǣ'rner haa leeterr behnsseen
Fill it up, please.	Full tank, er De snill.	fewl tahnk ǣr dee snil.
Please check the oil and water.	Vil De være så snill å sjekke oljen og vannet.	vil dee vǣrer saw snil aw shekker olyern o vahnner
Give me half a litre of oil.	Gi meg en halv liter olje.	yee may ehn hahl leeterr olyer

143

Fill up the battery with distilled water.	**Vil De være så snill å fylle batteriet med destillert vann.**	vil dee **vææ**rer saw snil aw **few**ller bahttereeer mäy dehstill**äy**rt vahn
Check the brake fluid.	**Kan De sjekke brem-sevæsken?**	kahn dee **shek**ker brehm-ssersversskern
Put in some anti-freeze, please.	**Kan De fylle på litt frysevæske?**	kahn dee **few**ller paw lit **frew**sservehssker

Fluid measures					
litres	imp. gal.	U.S. gal.	litres	imp. gal.	U.S. gal.
5	1.1	1.3	30	6.6	7.8
10	2.2	2.6	35	7.7	9.1
15	3.3	3.9	40	8.8	10.4
20	4.4	5.2	45	9.9	11.7
25	5.5	6.5	50	11.0	13.0

Would you please change this tire?	**Kunne De være så snill å skifte dette dekket?**	kewnner dee **vææ**rer saw snil aw **shif**ter **deht**ter **dehk**ker
Would you check the tires?	**Kan De sjekke dekkene?**	kahn dee **shek**ker **dehk**kerner
1.6 front, 1.8 rear.	**1 komma 6 foran, 1 komma 8 bak.**	1 **kom**mah 6 forahn, 1 **kom**mah 8 baak

Tire pressure is measured in Norway in kilograms per square centimetre. The following conversion chart will get your tires the treatment they deserve. Just point to the pressures required.

Tire pressure			
lb./sq. in.	kg./cm.^{2}	lb./sq. in.	kg./cm.^{2}
10	0.7	26	1.8
12	0.8	27	1.9
15	1.1	28	2.0
18	1.3	30	2.1
20	1.4	33	2.3
21	1.5	36	2.5
23	1.6	38	2.7
24	1.7	40	2.8

CAR-FILLING STATION

144

English	Norwegian	Pronunciation
Would you clean the windscreen (windshield)?	Vil De tørke av frontruten?	vil dee turrker ahv frontrewtern
I want maintenance and lubrication service.	Jeg vil ha vedlikehold og smøring.	yay vil haa vaydleekerholl o smūrring
Have you a road map of this district?	Har De et veikart over dette distriktet?	haar dee eht vaykah't avverr dehtter disstrikter
I've run out of petrol (gas) at... Could you please help me?	Jeg har sluppet opp for bensin ved... Kunne De være så snill å hjelpe meg?	yay haar sleuppert op for behnsseen vay... kewnner dee vǣrer saw snil aw yehlper may

Asking the way—Street directions

In large cities you'll be best off if you can produce a street plan and have somebody point out the way to go. However, here are some questions you will find useful:

English	Norwegian	Pronunciation
Excuse me. Do you speak English?	Unnskyld, snakker De engelsk?	ewnshewl, snahkkerr dee ehngerlsk
Can you tell me the way to...?	Kan De si meg veien til...?	kahn dee see may vayern til
Where's...?	Hvor er...?	voor ǣr
Where does this road lead to?	Hvor går denne veien?	voor gawr dehnner vayern

Miles into kilometres

1 mile = 1.609 kilometres (km.)

miles	10	20	30	40	50	60	70	80	90	100
km.	16	32	48	64	80	97	113	129	145	161

Kilometres into miles

1 kilometre (km. = 0.62 miles)

km.	10	20	30	40	50	60	70	80	90	100	110	120	130
miles	6	12	19	25	31	37	44	50	56	62	68	75	81

English	Norwegian	Pronunciation
Are we on the right road for...?	Er vi på rett vei til...?	ær vee paw reht vay til
How far is the next village?	Hvor langt er det til neste landsby?	voor lahngt ær day til nehsster lahnssbew
How far is it to... from here?	Hvor langt er det til...herfra?	voor lahngt ær day til...hærfrah
Can you tell me where...is?	Kan De si meg hvor...er?	kahn dee see may voor...ær
Where can I find this address?	Hvor kan jeg finne denne adressen?	voor kahn yay finner dehnner ahdrehssern
Where is this?	Hvor er dette?	voor ær dehtter
Can you show me on the map where I am?	Kan De vise meg på kartet hvor jeg er?	kahn dee veesser may paw kah'ter voor yay ær
Can you show me on the map where...is?	Kan De vise meg på kartet hvor...er?	kahn dee veesser may paw kah'ter voor...ær
Can I park there?	Kan jeg parkere der?	kahn yay pahrkayrer dær
Is that a one-way street?	Er dette en enveis-gate?	ær dehtter ehn aynvayss-gaater
Does the traffic go this way?	Går trafikken denne veien?	gawr trahfikkern dehnner vayern

De er på feil vei.	You're on the wrong road.
Kjør rett frem.	Go straight ahead.
Det er der nede til...	It's down there on the...
venstre/høyre	left/right
Det er for langt å gå.	It's too far to walk.
Ta buss nr...	Catch bus number...
Kjør til første/andre kryss.	Go to the first/second crossroads.
Ta til venstre ved trafikklysene.	Turn left at the traffic lights.
Ta til høyre ved hjørnet.	Turn right at the corner.

Part B

Customs—Documentation

To enter Norway with your car you must have the following documents:

passport
international insurance certificate (green card)
log book (vehicle registration card)
valid driving licence

Nationality sticker must be displayed on the rear of your car.

If you intend to stay in Norway more than three months, consult an automobile association at home for details of further requirements.

In Norway traffic drives on the right, passing on the left. Crash helmets are compulsory for riders and passengers on motor cycles and scooters.

It's advisable to have a red warning triangle and a separate parking lamp along with you, too.

Here's my...	Her er mitt...	hǣr ǣr mit
(international) driving licence	(internasjonale) bilsertifikat	(interrnahshōōnaaler) beelsæ'tifikaat
green card	grønne kort	grurnner ko't
log book (registration card)	vognkort	vongnko't
passport	pass	pahss
I've nothing to declare.	Jeg har ingenting å fortolle.	yay hahr ingernting aw fo'toller
I've...	Jeg har...	yay haar
a carton of cigarettes	en kartong sigaretter	ehn kah'tong siggahrehtterr
a bottle of whisky	en flaske whisky	ehn flahssker "whisky"
a bottle of wine	en flaske vin	ehn flahssker veen
We're staying for...	Vi skal være her i...	vee skahl vǣrer hǣr ee
a week	en uke	ehn ēwker
two weeks	to uker	too ēwkerr
a month	en måned	ehn mawnerd

CAR—INFORMATION

Roads and driving conditions

A glance at a map will illustrate the problems Norwegian road-builders face: rugged mountainous terrain, raging torrents, a deeply indented coastline—all compounded by severe winters in the interior of the country (the coast remains relatively mild).

Taking all these natural obstacles into account, Norway's roads are fairly good. And close to the major towns they improve noticeably.

If you want to enjoy the scenery—and practically all parts of the country offer impressive views and charming drives —don't try to fit too much into each day. A hundred and fifty miles per day would leave you time to enjoy your drive.

If you really have to cover long distances rapidly you will be greatly helped, in summer, by the very long hours of daylight. As is well known, the north of the country enjoys twenty-four hours of daylight in summer, and even in the south it doesn't get really dark in June and July until around 11 o'clock at night. However, drivers tend to use their side-lights, and often even dipped headlights, during the long twilight hours.

In winter, of course, you'll see the other side of the coin: the days, then, are as short as the nights were in winter, and in the far north there's very little daylight at all.

There are a few motorways (*motorveier*—**mōō**toorvayerr). More common are the main highways (*riksveier*—**riks**vayerr) connecting towns and villages. You will also encounter *fylkesveier* (**fewl**kerssvayerr), less-travelled roads, not always paved.

In the fjord country and northern Norway, car ferries provide interesting breaks in the driving routine. In the north, there's often no road round a fjord in any case, so you're forced to take the ferry.

For longer crossings it's a good idea to book space in advance on the ferries. Hotel porters can handle this for you.

From October to the end of May or the beginning of June, several mountain roads are blocked by snow. The Norwegian Automobile Association in Oslo can provide timely information.

Year-round mountain roads, always clear, are the E68 across the Filefjell mountain to the Sognefjord, and E76 across the Haukeli mountain to the Hardangerfjord.

The speed limits are:

80 km/h (approx. 50 mph) on the open road;
50 km/h (approx. 30 mph) in built-up areas.

Heavy fines face any driver—even a tourist—exceeding these strict limits. The traffic police are extremely vigilant.

I'm sorry, Officer, I didn't see the sign/ light.	Jeg beklager, jeg så ikke skiltet/ lyset.	yay ber**klaa**ger, yay saw **i**kker shilter/ **lew**sser
The light was green.	Lyset var grønt.	**lew**sser vahr grurnt

Parking

In Oslo and other big towns it's quite difficult to find parking space for longer stays. However, there are plenty of meters both in the centre and in the outskirts of the towns. Be careful not to exceed the time limit, as the traffic wardens are constantly on patrol.

Excuse me. May I park here?	Unnskyld, kan jeg parkere her?	**ewn**shewl, kahn yay pahr**kay**rer h**ær**
How long may I park here?	Hvor lenge kan jeg stå her?	voor **leh**nger kahn yay staw h**ær**
What's the charge for parking here?	Hva koster det å parkere her?	vah **koss**terr d**ay** aw pahr**kay**rer h**ær**
Do I have to leave my lights on?	Må jeg la lysene stå på?	maw yay laa **lew**sserner staw paw
Excuse me. Do you have some change for the parking meter?	Unnskyld, kan De veksle noen småpenger til parkometeret?	**ewn**shewl, kahn dee **vehks**ler **noo**ern **smaw**pehngerr til pahrkoo**may**terrer

Norwegian road signs

In addition to the internationally standardized road signs (see pages 160-161), Norway uses some signs and notices of its own, sometimes in conjunction with pictographs, sometimes alone. Study this page beforehand so you're prepared for them.

DÅRLIG VEI (VEG)	Bad road
FARE	Danger
FOTGJENGERFELT	Pedestrian crossing
GRUSVEI	Gravelled road
GÅGATE	Pedestrian path
HOLD TIL HØYRE	Keep right
KJØR LANGSOMT	Drive slowly
OMKJØRING	Diversion (detour)
PARKERING FORBUDT	No parking
PARKERINGSOMRÅDE	Parking lot
PRIVAT PARKERING	Private parking only
RASFARE	Avalanche area, falling rocks
SKOLE	School
SMAL/GLATT/SVINGET VEI (VEG)	Narrow/Slippery/Winding road
SONE	Zone
SPRENGNING PÅGÅR, SLÅ AV RADIOSENDER	Blasting taking place, switch off radio transmitter
STOPP, POLITI	Stop, police
TELELØSNING/TELELØYSE	Pot-hole (due to frost)
TENN LYSET	Use headlights
TOLL	Customs
UTKJØRSEL	Lorry (truck) exit
VEIARBEID (VEGARBEID) PÅGÅR	Road under repair

CAR—INFORMATION

FOR INTERNATIONAL ROAD SIGNS, see pages 160-161

Part C

Accidents

This section is confined to immediate aid. The legal problems of responsibility and settlement can be taken care of at a later stage. Your first concern will be for the injured.

Is anyone hurt?	Er noen skadet?	ær nŏŏern skaadert
Don't move!	Ikke rør Dem!	ikker rūrr dehm
It's all right, don't worry.	Alt er i orden. Ingen fare.	ahlt ær ee ordern ingern faarer
Where's the nearest telephone?	Hvor er nærmeste telefon?	voor ær nærmehsster tehlehfŏŏn
Can I use your phone? There's been an accident.	Kan jeg få låne telefonen Deres? Det har skjedd en ulykke.	kahn yay faw lawner tehlehfŏŏnern dāyrerss. dāy haar shehd ehn ēwlewkker
Call a doctor/an ambulance quickly.	Ring etter lege/ sykebil så fort som mulig.	ring ehtterr lāyger/ sēwkerbeel saw foo't som mēwli
There are people injured.	Det er noen som er skadet.	dāy ær nŏŏern som ær skaadert
Help me get them out of the car.	Hjelp meg å få dem ut av bilen!	yehlp may aw faw dehm ēwt ahv beelern

Police—Exchange of information

Please call the police.	Vær så snill og ring politiet!	vær saw snil o ring pooliteeer
There's been an accident.	Det har skjedd en ulykke.	dāy haar shehd ehn ēwlewkker
It's about 2 kilometres from...	Det er ca. 2 kilometer fra...	dāy ær sirkah 2 kheeloomāyterr frah
I'm on the Oslo-Drammen road, 25 kilometres from Drammen.	Jeg er på veien mellom Oslo-Drammen, 25 kilometer fra Drammen.	yay ær paw vayern mehllom oossloodrahmmern, 25 kheeloomāyterr frah drahmmern
Here's my name and address.	Her er mitt navn og adresse.	hær ær mit nahvn o ahdrehsser

CAR-REPAIRS

| Would you mind acting as a witness? | **Har De noe imot å være vitne?** | haar dee nōōer eemoot aw værrer vitner |
| I'd like an interpreter. | **Jeg vil gjerne ha en tolk.** | yay vil yǣr'ner haa ehn tolk |

Remember to put out a red warning triangle if your car is out of action or impeding traffic.

Breakdown

...and that's what we'll do with this section: break it down into four phases.

1. *On the road*
   You ask where the nearest garage is.

2. *At the garage*
   You tell the mechanic what's wrong.

3. *Finding the trouble*
   He tells you what he thinks needs doing.

4. *Getting it repaired*
   You tell him to repair it and, once that's over, settle the account (or argue about it).

Phase 1—On the road

Where's the nearest garage?	**Hvor ligger nærmeste bilverksted?**	voor liggerr nærmehsster beelværkssteh
Excuse me, my car has broken down. May I use your phone?	**Unnskyld, men bilen min har fått motorstopp. Kan jeg få låne telefonen?**	ewnshewl, mehn beelern meen hahr fawt mōōtoorstop. kahn yay faw lawner tehlehfōōnern
What's the telephone number of the nearest garage?	**Hva er telefonnummeret til nærmeste bilverksted?**	vah ær tehlehfōōnnoommerrer til nærmehsster beelværkssteh
I've had a breakdown at...	**Jeg har fått motorstopp ved...**	yay hahr fawt mōōtoorstop vāy
We're on the Oslo-Hamar motorway (expressway) about 10 kilometres from Hamar.	**Vi er på motorveien Oslo-Hamar ca. 10 km fra Hamar.**	vee ær paw mōōtoorvayern oossloo haamahr sirkah 10 kheeloomāyterr frah haamahr

Can you send a mechanic?	Kan De sende en mekaniker?	kahn dee **sehn**ner ehn meh**kaan**ikkerr
Can you send a truck to tow my car?	Kan De sende en kranvogn til å taue bilen min?	kahn dee **sehn**ner ehn **kraan**vongn til aw **tower** beelern meen
How long will you be?	Hvor lang tid vil det ta?	voor lahng teed vil dāy taa

Phase 2—At the garage

I don't know what's wrong with it.	Jeg vet ikke hva som er i veien med den.	yay vāyt ikker vah som ǣr ee **vay**ern māy dehn
I think there's something wrong with the...	Jeg tror det er noe galt med...	yay troor dāy ǣr **nōō**er gaalt māy
acceleration	akselerasjonen	ahksehlehrah**shōō**nern
axle	akselen	**ahks**erlern
battery	batteriet	bahtterreeer
brakes	bremsene	**brehms**serner
choke	choken	**shōō**kern
clutch	clutchen	**klurts**hern
cooling system	kjøleanlegget	**khūr**lerahnlehgger
dip (dimmer) switch	avblenderen	**ahv**blehnderrern
direction indicator	blinklyset	**blink**lēwsser
distributor	fordeleren	for**dāy**lehrern
door	døren	**dūr**rern
dynamo	dynamoen	dewnaa**moo**ern
engine	motoren	**mōō**toorern
exhaust system	eksosanlegget	ehk**sōō**ssahnlehgger
fan	viften	**vif**tern
fan belt	vifteremmen	**vif**terrehmmern
fuel feed	bensintilførselen	behn**sseen**tilfursherlern
gears	gearet	**gee**erer
generator	dynamoen	dewnaa**moo**ern
heating	oppvarmingen	**op**vahrmingern
horn	hornet	**hōō**'ner
ignition system	tenningen	**tehn**ningern
injection system	innsprøytingen	**in**sproytingern
lights	lysene	**lēws**serne
brake lights	bremselysene	brehmsser**lēws**sserner
headlights	hovedlysene	hōōverd**lēws**sserner

rear (tail) lights	baklysene	baak<u>lew</u>sserner
reversing (backup) lights	ryggelysene	rewgger<u>lew</u>sserner
muffler	lydpotten	<u>lew</u>dpottern
oil system	oljesystemet	olyerssewsst<u>ay</u>mer
overdrive	overgearet	<u>aw</u>vehrgeerer
radiator	radiatoren	rahdi<u>aa</u>toorern
seat	setet	s<u>ay</u>ter
seat belt	sikkerhetsbeltet	sikkerrh<u>ay</u>tsbehlter
silencer	lydpotten	<u>lew</u>dpottern
speedometer	speedometeret	speedom<u>ay</u>terrer
starter motor	starteren	staa'terrern
steering	styringen	st<u>ew</u>ringern
suspension	fjæringen	fy<u>ææ</u>ringern
transmission	gearkassen	geerkahssern
turn signal	blinklysene	blink<u>lew</u>sserner
wheels	hjulene	y<u>ew</u>lerner
wipers	vinduspusserne	vindewsspewssæ'ner

LEFT	RIGHT
VENSTRE	**HØYRE**
(vehnsstrer)	(hoyrer)

FRONT	BACK
FORAN	**BAK**
(forahn)	(baak)

It's...

backfiring	ettertenner	ehtterrtehnnerr
bad	dårlig	daw'li
blowing	lekk	lehk
blown	ødelagt	<u>ur</u>derlahgt
broken	gått i stykker	got ee st<u>ew</u>kkerr
burnt	brent	brehnt
chafing	blir varm	bleer vahrm
cracked	sprukket	sprookkert
defective	defekt	dehfehkt
disconnected	frakoplet	fraakoplert
dry	tørt	tur't
frozen	frosset	frossert
jammed	sitter fast	sitterr fahsst
jerking	rykker	rewkkerr
knocking	banker	bahnkerr
leaking	lekker	lehkkerr
loose	løst	l<u>ur</u>sst

noisy	**bråker**	brawkerr
overheating	**blir for varm**	bleer for vahrm
slack	**løst**	lūrsst
slipping	**glir**	gleer
split	**revner**	rehvnerr
stuck	**sitter fast**	sitterr fahsst
vibrating	**vibrerer**	vibra̅yrerr
weak	**svakt**	svaakt

The car won't start.	**Bilen vil ikke starte.**	beelern vil ikker stah'ter
The car won't pull.	**Bilen vil ikke dra.**	beelern vil ikker draa
The car is making a funny noise.	**Bilen har en rar lyd.**	beelern haar ehn raar le̅wd
It's locked and the keys are inside.	**Denn er låst og nøklene er inni.**	dehn a̅er lawst o nurklerner a̅er inni
The radiator is leaking.	**Radiatoren lekker.**	rahdiaatoorern lehkkerr
The clutch engages too quickly.	**Clutchen tar for fort.**	klurtshern taar for foo'rt
I can't engage first/reverse gear.	**Jeg får den ikke i første gear/revers.**	yay fawr dehn ikker ee furshter geer/rehvæsh
The steering wheel's vibrating.	**Rattet vibrerer.**	rahtter vibra̅yrerr
The...needs adjusting.	**...trenger justering.**	...trehngerr yewssta̅yring
brake/clutch idling	**bremsen/clutchen/ tomgangen**	brehmssern/klurtshern/ tomgahngern

Now that you've explained what's wrong, you'll want to know how long it'll take to repair it and make your arrangements accordingly.

How long will it take to find out what's wrong?	**Hvor lang tid tar det å finne ut hva som er galt?**	voor lahng teed taar da̅y aw finner e̅wt vah som a̅er gaalt
How long will it take to repair?	**Hvor lang tid tar reparasjonen?**	voor lahng teed taar rehpahrahsho̅onern
Suppose I come back in half an hour?	**Kan jeg komme tilbake om en halv time?**	kahn yay kommer tilbaaker om ehn hahl teemer

Can you give me a lift into town?	Kan jeg få sitte på inn til byen?	kahn yay faw **sitter** paw in til b**ew**ern
Is there a place to stay nearby?	Finnes det et sted jeg kan ta inn i nærheten?	**finners** d**a**y eht st**a**yd yay kahn tah in ee n**ae**rhehtern
May I use your phone?	Kan jeg få låne telefonen Deres?	kahn yay faw **lawner** tehlehf**oo**nern d**a**yress

Phase 3—Finding the trouble

Now it's up to the mechanic to pinpoint the trouble and repair it. Just hand him the book and point to the text in Norwegian below.

Vennligst se på den alfabetiske listen som følger, og pek på delen som er ødelagt. Hvis kunden Deres vil vite hva som er i veien med den, ta ut det rette uttrykket fra den påfølgende listen (brukket, kortsluttet etc.). *

aksel	shaft
batteri	battery
battericeller	battery cells
batterivæske	battery fluid
beholder	casing
bensinmåler	fuel gauge
-pumpe	pump
-tank	tank
-tilførsel	feed
blanding	mixture
bolt	bolt
brems	brake
bremsebelegg	brake lining
bremsesko	brake shoes
bremsetrommel	brake drum
børster	brushes
choke	choke
clutch	clutch
clutchpedal	clutch pedal
clutchplate	clutch plate
coil	coil
dimbryter	dip (dimmer) switch
dynamo	dynamo (generator)

* Please look at the following alphabetical list and point to the defective item. If your customer wants to know what's wrong with it, pick the applicable term from the next list (broken, short-circuited etc.).

elektrisk anlegg	electrical system
feste	mountings
filter	filter
fjær	spring
fjæring	suspension
flottør	float
fordeler	distributor
fordelerledere	distributor leads
forgasser	carburettor
forgreningsrør	manifold
forgreningsrørpakning	manifold gasket
fôring (clutch)	lining (clutch)
gearkasse	gear box
gearoverføring	transmission
gearstang	gear lever
hjul	wheels
hjulstilling	tracking
hovedlager	main bearing
hydraulisk bremseanlegg	hydraulic brake system
innsprøytningspumpe	injection pump
kabel	cable
kamaksel	camshaft
kardang	differential
kjøleanlegg	cooling system
kondensator	condenser
kontakt	contact
kopling	connection
kronhjul og pinjong	crown wheel and pinion
lager	bearing
ledere	leads
ledning	wire
ledningsnett	wiring
luftfilter	air filter
lydpotte	silencer (muffler)
mellomaksel	propeller shaft
membran	diaphragm
motor	engine
motorblokk	block
måler	gauge
pakning	joint, gasket (packing)
pumpe	pump
radiator	radiator
rattsøyle	steering column (post)
reflektor	reflector
relé	relay
rotor	rotor arm
selvstarterdrev	starter armature

CAR-REPAIRS

stabilisatorstag	stabilizer
startmotor	starter motor
stempel	piston
stempelfjær	ring
stifter	points
styresnekke	steering-box
styring	steering
støtdemper	shock-absorber
svinghjul	flywheel
sylinder	cylinder
tannstag og pinjong	rack and pinion
tenner	teeth
tenningsjustering	timing
tennplugger	sparking-plugs
termostat	thermostat
topplokk	cylinder head
topplokk-pakning	cylinder head gasket
understell	chassis
universalledd	universal joint
vannpumpe	water-pump
varsellampe	warning lamp
veivaksel	crankshaft
veivhus	crankcase
veivstang	connecting (piston) rod
ventil	valve
vifte	fan
vifterem	fan-belt

Følgende liste inneholder ord som forklarer hva som er galt eller hva som må gjøres med bilen.*

balansere	to balance
brent	burnt
defekt	defective
demontere	to strip down
fet blanding	rich
frakoplet	disconnected
frosset	frozen
fusker	misfiring
glipper	slipping
går for varm	overheating
gått i stykker	broken
hurtig	quick, fast
innstille	to adjust

* The following list contains words which describe what's wrong as well as what may need to be done.

justere	to adjust
klaring	play
klemt fast	jammed
korrodert	corroded
kortsluttet	short-circuited
lade	to charge
lader ikke	not charging
lavt	low
lekker	leaking, blowing
lufte	to bleed
løst	loose
løsne	to loosen
slakt	slack
oksydert	pitted
raskt	quick, fast
skifte	to change
skifte ut	to replace
skittent	dirty
slipe	to grind in
sprukket	cracked
stramme	to tighten
svakt	weak
tørt	dry
utslitt	worn
vaske	to clean
ødelagt	blown

Phase 4—Getting it repaired

Have you found the trouble?	Har De funnet feilen?	haar dee fewnnert faylern
Is that serious?	Er det alvorlig?	ær day ahlvo'li
Can you repair it?	Kan De reparere det?	kahn dee rehpahrayrer day
Can you do it now?	Kan De gjøre det nå?	kahn dee yūrrer day naw
What's it going to cost?	Hva kommer det til å koste?	vah kommerr day til aw kosster

What if he says "no"?

Why can't you do it?	Hvorfor kan De ikke gjøre det?	voorfor kahn dee ikker yūrrer day
Is it essential to have that part?	Er det helt nødvendig å ha den delen?	ær day haylt nurdvehndi aw haa dehn daylern

How long is it going to take to get the spare parts?	**Hvor lang tid vil det ta å få tak i reservedelene?**	voor lahng teed vil dāy taa aw faw taak ee rehsærver-dāylerner
Where's the nearest garage that can repair it?	**Hvor er nærmeste verksted som kan reparere det?**	voor ār nærmehsster værk-stāy som kahn rehpahrāy-rer dāy
Can you fix it so that I can get as far as...?	**Kan De fikse det så jeg kan komme så langt som til...?**	kahn dee fikser dāy saw yay kahn kommer saw lahngt som til

If you're really stuck, ask:

| Can I leave my car here for a day/a few days? | **Kan jeg la bilen stå her en dag/ noen få dager?** | kahn yay laa beelern staw hār ehn daag/ nōōern faw daagerr |

Settling the bill

Is everything fixed?	**Er alt ordnet?**	ār ahlt ordnert
How much do I owe you?	**Hvor mye skylder jeg Dem?**	voor mēwer shewllerr yay dehm
Will you take a traveller's cheque?	**Kan De ta en reise-sjekk?**	kahn dee taa ehn raysser-shehk
Thanks very much for your help.	**Tusen takk for hjelpen.**	tēwssern tahk for yehlpern
This is for you.	**Dette er til Dem.**	dehtter ār til dehm

But you may feel that the workmanship is sloppy or that you're paying for work not done. Get the bill itemized.

If necessary, get it translated before you pay.

| I'd like to check the bill first. | **Jeg vil gjerne sjekke regningen først.** | yay vil yǣrner shekker rayningen fursht |
| Will you itemize the work done? | **Vil De spesifisere arbeidet?** | vil dee spehssifisāyrer ahrbayder |

If the garage still won't back down, and you're sure you're right, get the help of a third party.

Some international road signs

No vehicles

No entry

No overtaking (passing)

Oncoming traffic has priority

Maximum speed limit

No parking

Caution

Intersection

Dangerous bend (curve)

Road narrows

Intersection with secondary road

Two-way traffic

Dangerous hill

Uneven road

Falling rocks

Give way (yield)

Main road,
thoroughfare

End of restriction

One-way traffic

Traffic goes
this way

Roundabout
(rotary)

Bicycles only

Pedestrians
only

Minimum speed
limit

Keep right
(left if symbol
reversed)

Parking

Hospital

Motorway
(expressway)

Motor vehicles
only

Filling station

No through road

Doctor

Frankly, how much use is a phrase book going to be to you in case of serious injury or illness? The only phrase you need in such an emergency is...

| Get a doctor, quick! | **Hent en lege, fort!** | hehnt ehn **lāy**ger foo't |

But there are minor aches and pains, ailments and irritations that can upset the best-planned trip. Here we can help you and, perhaps, the doctor.

Some doctors will speak English well; others will know enough for your needs. But suppose there's something the doctor can't explain because of language difficulties? We've thought of that. As you'll see, this section has been arranged to enable you and the doctor to communicate. From page 165 to 171, you'll find your part of the dialogue on the upper half of each page—the doctor's is on the lower half.

The whole section has been divided into three parts: illness, wounds, nervous tension. Page 171 is concerned with prescriptions and fees.

General

Can you get me a doctor?	**Kan De skaffe meg en lege?**	kahn dee **skahf**fer may ehn **lāy**ger
Is there a doctor here?	**Er det en lege her?**	ǣr dāy ehn **lay**ger hǣr
Please telephone for a doctor immediately.	**Vær så snill og ring etter en lege med en gang.**	vǣr saw snil o ring **eht**terr ehn **lāy**ger māy **ayn** gahng
Where's there a doctor who speaks English?	**Hvor finnes en lege som snakker engelsk?**	voor **finn**ers ehn **lāy**ger som **snahk**kerr **ehng**erlsk
Where's the surgery (doctor's office)?	**Hvor er legekontoret?**	voor ǣr **lāy**gerkoontōōrer

FOR CHEMIST'S, see page 108

What are the surgery (office) hours?	**Når har legen kontortid?**	nawr haar **lāy**gern koon**tōōr**teed
Could the doctor come to see me here?	**Kan legen komme hit og undersøke meg?**	kahn **lāy**gern **kom**mer heet o **ewn**nerrssūrker may
What time can the doctor come?	**Når kan legen komme?**	nawr kahn **lāy**gern **kom**mer

Symptoms

Use this section to tell the doctor what's wrong. Basically, what he'll require to know is:

What?	(ache, pain, bruise etc.)
Where?	(arm, stomach etc.)
How long?	(have you had the trouble)

Before you visit the doctor find out the answers to these questions by glancing through the pages that follow. In this way, you'll save time.

DOCTOR

Parts of the body

ankle	ankel	**ahn**kerl
appendix	blindtarm	**blinn**tahrm
arm	arm	ahrm
artery	arterie	ahr**tāy**reeer
back	rygg	rewg
bladder	blære	**blæ**rer
blood	blod	blōō
bone	ben	bāyn
breast	bryst	brewsst
cheek	kinn	khin
chest	brystkasse	**brewsst**kahsser
chin	hake	**haa**ker
collar-bone	kraveben	**kraa**verbāyn
ear	øre	**ūr**rer
elbow	albue	ahl**bew**er
eye	øye	**oy**er
face	ansikt	**ahn**sikt
finger	finger	**fing**err
foot	fot	fōōt
forehead	panne	**pahn**ner
gland	kjertel	**khæ**'terl

hand	hånd	hon
head	hode	hōōder
heart	hjerte	yæ'ter
heel	hæl	hāyl
hip	hofte	hofter
intestines	tarmer	tahrmerr
jaw	kjeve	khāyver
joint	ledd	lehd
kidney	nyre	nēwrer
knee	kne	knāy
knuckle	knoke	knōōker
leg	ben	bāyn
ligament	sene	sāyner
lip	leppe	lehpper
liver	lever	lehverr
lung	lunge	loonger
mouth	munn	mewn
muscle	muskel	mewsskerl
neck	nakke	nahkker
nerve	nerve	nærver
nervous system	nervesystem	nærverssewsstāym
nose	nese	nāysser
pelvis	bekken	behkkern
rectum	rectum	rehktewm
rib	ribben	ribbāyn
shoulder	skulder	skewllderr
sinus	bihule	beehēwler
skin	hud	hēwd
spine	ryggrad	rewgraad
stomach	mage	maager
tendon	sene	sāyner
thigh	lår	lawr
throat	hals	hahlss
thumb	tommel	tommerl
toe	tå	taw
tongue	tunge	toonger
tonsils	mandler	mahndlerr
urine	urin	ēwreen
vein	vene	vāyner
wrist	håndledd	hawnlerd

LEFT	RIGHT
VENSTRE	**HØYRE**
(vehnsstrer)	(hoyrer)

PATIENT
Part 1—Illness

I'm not feeling well.	**Jeg føler meg ikke bra.**	yay fūrlerr may ikker braa
I'm ill.	**Jeg er dårlig.**	yay ǣr daw'li
I've got a pain here.	**Jeg har vondt her.**	yay haar voont hǣr
My/His/Her...hurts.	**Mitt/Hans/ Hennes...gjør vondt.**	mit/hahnss/ hehnnerss...yūr voont
I've/He's/She's got (a)...	**Jeg/han/hun har...**	yay/hahn/hewn haar
backache	**vondt i ryggen**	voont ee rewggern
fever	**feber**	fāyberr
headache	**vondt i hodet**	voont ee hōōder
sore throat	**vondt i halsen**	voont ee hahlssern
stomach ache	**vondt i magen**	voont ee maagern
I'm constipated.	**Jeg har forstoppelse.**	yay haar foshtopperlsser
I've a bad cough.	**Jeg har en stygg hoste.**	yay haar ehn stewg hoosster
I've been vomiting.	**Jeg har kastet opp.**	yay haar kahsstert op

---

DOCTOR
1—Sykdom

Hva er i veien?	What's the trouble?
Hvor gjør det vondt?	Where does it hurt?
Hva slags smerte er det?	What sort of pain is it?
uklar/skarp/bankende konstant/nå og da	dull/sharp/throbbing constant/on and off
Hvor lenge har De hatt denne smerten?	How long have you had this pain?
Hvor lenge har De følt Dem slik?	How long have you been feeling like this?
Trekk opp ermet!	Roll up your sleeve.
Vil De være så vennlig å kle av Dem til livet.	Please undress to the waist.

DOCTOR

PATIENT

I feel...	**Jeg føler meg...**	yay fūrlerr may
faint/dizzy/ nauseous	**svimmel / svak / kvalm**	**svimm**erl / svaak / kvahlm
I feel shivery.	**Jeg har kuldegys- ninger.**	yay haar **kull**er**yew**ss- ningerr
I've/He's/She's got (a/an)...	**Jeg / Han / Hun har...**	yay / hahn / hewn haar
abscess	**en svull**	ehn svewl
asthma	**astma**	**ahs**tmah
boil	**en byll**	ehn bewl
chill	**snue**	**snew**er
cold	**blitt forkjølet**	blit for**khur**lert
constipation	**forstoppelse**	fosh**top**perlsser
cramps	**kramper**	**krahm**perr
diarrhoea	**diaré**	deeah**ray**
fever	**feber**	**fay**berr
haemorrhoids	**hemorroider**	hehmoorroo**ee**derr
hay fever	**høysnue**	**hoy**snewer

DOCTOR

Legg Dem ned her.	Please lie down over here.
Lukk opp munnen.	Open your mouth.
Pust dypt.	Breathe deeply.
Host.	Cough, please.
Gjør dette vondt?	Does this hurt?
Jeg skal måle temperaturen Deres.	I'll take your temperature.
Er det første gang De har hatt dette?	Is this the first time you've had this?
Jeg vil ha en urinprøve / avføringsprøve.	I want a sample of your urine/ stools.
Hvilken blodtype har De?	What is your blood type?

DOCTOR

PATIENT

hernia	**brokk**	brok
indigestion	**dårlig fordøyelse**	**daw'li fo'doyer**lsser
inflammation of...	**betennelse i...**	be**tehn**nerlsser ee
influenza	**influensa**	inf**lewehn**ssah
measles	**meslinger**	**mehss**lingerr
morning sickness	**morgenkvalme**	**maw**ernkvahlmer
rheumatism	**reumatisme**	row**mahtiss**mer
stiff neck	**stiv nakke**	steev **nahk**ker
sunstroke	**solstikk**	**sōōl**stik
tonsillitis	**betente mandler**	be**tehn**ter **mahnd**lerr
ulcer	**verksår**	**vӕӕrk**sawr
whooping cough	**kikhoste**	**khik**hoosster
It's nothing serious, I hope?	**Det er ikke noe alvorlig, håper jeg?**	dāy ӕr ikker **nōō**er ahl**vo'**li **haw**perr yay
I'd like you to prescribe some medicine for me.	**Jeg vil gjerne at De skriver ut noe medisin til meg.**	yay vil **yӕӕ'**ner aht dee **skree**verr ēwt **nōō**er meh**dis**seen til may

DOCTOR

DOCTOR

Det er ikke noe å bry seg om. — It's nothing to worry about.

De må holde sengen i ...dager. — You must stay in bed for...days.

De har... — You've got (a/an)...

betennelse i...	inflammation of...
blindtarmbetennelse	appendicitis
forkjølelse	cold
influensa	influenza
leddgikt	arthritis
matforgiftning	food poisoning
verksår	ulcer

Jeg vil gjerne at De drar til sykehuset til en rutine-undersøkelse. — I want you to go to the hospital for a general check-up.

Jeg skal skrive ut en resept på et antibiotikum. — I'll prescribe an antibiotic.

PATIENT

I'm a diabetic.	**Jeg er diabetiker.**	yay **ǣr** deeahbⓐ̄yteekerr
I've a cardiac condition.	**Jeg har svakt hjerte.**	yay haar svaakt **yǣ'**ter
I had a heart attack in...	**Jeg hadde et hjerte-anfall i...**	yay **hahd**der eht **yǣ'**ter-ahnfahl ee
I'm allergic to...	**Jeg er allergisk mot...**	yay **ǣr** ahl**lǣr**gisk moot
This is my usual medicine.	**Dette er min vanlige medisin.**	**deht**ter **ǣr** meen **vaan**leeer mehdee**sseen**
I need this medicine.	**Jeg trenger denne medisinen.**	yay **trehng**err **dehn**ner mehdee**sseen**ern
I'm expecting a baby.	**Jeg er gravid.**	yay **ǣr** grah**veed**
Can I travel?	**Kan jeg reise?**	kahn y**ā̄y rays**serr

DOCTOR

Hvor mye insulin pleier De å ta?	What dose of insulin are you taking?
Som sprøyte eller tabletter?	Injection or oral?
Hvilken behandling har De fått?	What treatment have you been having?
Hvilken medisin har De tatt?	What medicine have you been taking?
Har De noen gang hatt ubehag av penicillin?	Have you ever had ill effects from penicillin?
De har hatt et (lett) hjerteanfall.	You've had a (slight) heart attack.
Vi bruker ikke...i Norge. Dette er omtrent det samme.	We don't use...in Norway. This is very similar.
Når venter De barnet?	When's the baby due.
De kan ikke reise før...	You can't travel until...

PATIENT

Part 2—Wounds

Could you have a look at this...?	Kan De se på...	kahn dee sāy paw
blister	denne blemmen	dehnner blehmmern
boil	denne byllen	dehnner bewllern
bruise	denne skrammen	dehnner skrahmmern
burn	denne forbrenningen	dehnner forbrehnningern
cut	dette kuttet	dehtter kewtter
graze	dette skrubbsåret	dehtter skrewbsawrer
insect bite	dette insektstikket	dehtter insehktstikker
lump	denne klumpen	dehnner kloompern
rash	dette utslettet	dehtter ēwtslehtter
sting	dette stikket	dehtter stikker
swelling	denne hevelsen	dehnner hāyverlssern
wound	dette såret	dehtter sawrer
I can't move my...	Jeg kan ikke bevege...	yay kahn ikker behvāyger
It hurts.	Det gjør vondt.	dāy yūrr voont

DOCTOR

2—Skader, sår

Det er (ikke) betent.	It's (not) infected.
De har en skiveforskyvning.	You've got a slipped disc.
Jeg vil De skal ta et røntgen-bilde.	I want you to have an x-ray.
Er De blitt vaksinert mot stivkrampe? Når?	Have you been vaccinated against tetanus? When?
Det er...	It's...
brukket/forstuet	broken/sprained
gått av ledd/vrikket	dislocated/torn
De har forstrukket en muskel.	You've pulled a muscle.
Jeg skal gi Dem noe anti-septisk. Det er ikke alvorlig.	I'll give you an antiseptic. It's not serious.
Jeg vil at De skal komme igjen om...dager.	I want you to come and see me in...days' time.

DOCTOR

PATIENT

Part 3—Nervous tension

I'm in a nervous state.	Jeg føler meg nervøs.	yay fürlerr may nehrvürss
I'm feeling depressed.	Jeg føler meg deprimert.	yay fürlerr may dehprimāy't
I want some sleeping pills.	Jeg vil gjerne ha noen sovepiller.	yay vil yǣ'ner haa nōōern sawverpillerr
I can't eat.	Jeg orker ikke å spise.	yay orkerr ikker aw speesser
I can't sleep.	Jeg får ikke sove.	yay fawr ikker sawver
I'm having nightmares.	Jeg har mareritt.	yay haar maarerritt
Can you prescribe a/an...?	Kan De skrive ut noe...?	kahn dee skreever ēwt nōōer
tranquillizer	beroligende	behrōōleeggernder
anti-depressant	oppkvikkende	opkvikkehnder

DOCTOR

DOCTOR

3—Nervøse lidelser

De lider av nervøs anspenthet.	You're suffering from nervous tension.
De trenger hvile.	You need a rest.
Hvilke medisiner har De tatt?	What medicine have you been taking?
Hvor mange om dagen?	How many a day?
Hvor lenge har De følt Dem slik?	How long have you been feeling like this?
Jeg skal skrive ut noe medisin.	I'll prescribe some medicine.
Jeg skal gi Dem et beroligende middel.	I'll give you a tranquillizer.

PATIENT

Prescriptions and dosage

What kind of medicine is this?	**Hva slags medisin er dette?**	vah slahgss mehdi**sseen ær deht**ter
How many times a day should I take it?	**Hvor mange ganger om dagen skal jeg ta den?**	voor **mahng**er **gahng**err om **daa**gern skahl yay taa dehn
Must I swallow them whole?	**Må jeg svelge dem hele?**	maw yay **svehl**ger dehm **hay**ler

Fee

How much do I owe you?	**Hvor mye skylder jeg Dem?**	voor **mew**er **shewl**lerr yay dehm
Do I pay you now or will you send me your bill?	**Skal jeg betale Dem nå, eller vil De sende regningen?**	skahl yay ber**taal**er dehm naw **ehl**lerr vil dee **sehn**ner **rayn**ingern
May I have a receipt?	**Kan jeg få kvitte-ring?**	kahn yay faw kvit**tay**ring

---

DOCTOR

Resepter og dosering

Ta...teskjeer av denne medisinen hver...time.	Take...teaspoons of this medicine every...hours.
Ta...piller med et glass vann...	Take...pills with a glass of water...
...ganger om dagen	...times a day
før hvert måltid	before each meal
etter hvert måltid	after each meal
om morgenen	in the mornings
om kvelden	at night

Honorar

Vil De være så vennlig å betale meg nå.	Please pay me now.
Jeg sender Dem regningen.	I'll send you a bill.

FOR NUMBERS, see page 175

DOCTOR

Dentist

Can you recommend a good dentist?	**Kan De anbefale en god tannlege?**	kahn dee **ahn**berfaaler ehn gōō tahn**lay**ger
Can I make an (urgent) appointment to see Doctor...?	**Kan jeg få time (snarest) hos tann-lege...?**	kahn yay faw **tee**mer (snaarerst) hooss **tahn**layger
Can't you possibly make it earlier than that?	**Kan jeg ikke få noe før det?**	kahn yay **ikk**er faw **nōō**er furr day
I've got toothache.	**Jeg har tannpine.**	yay haar **tahn**peener
I've an abscess.	**Jeg har tannbyll.**	yay haar **tahn**bewl
This tooth hurts.	**Det gjør vondt i denne tannen.**	day yurr voont ee **dehn**ner **tahn**nern
at the top	**oppe**	**opp**er
at the bottom	**nede**	**nay**der
in the front	**foran**	**for**ahn
at the back	**bak**	baak
Can you fix it temporarily?	**Kan De reparere det midlertidig?**	kahn dee rehpah**ray**rer day midlerr**tee**di
I don't want it extracted.	**Jeg vil ikke at De skal trekke den.**	yay vil **ikk**er aht dee skahl **trehk**ker dehn
I've a loose tooth.	**Jeg har en løs tann.**	yay haar ehn lurss tahn
I've broken a tooth.	**Jeg har brukket en tann.**	yay haar **brokk**ert ehn tahn
I've lost a filling.	**Jeg har mistet en plombe.**	yay haar **miss**tert ehn **ploom**ber
The gum is very sore.	**Tannkjøttet er svært sårt.**	**tahn**khurtter ær svæ't saw't
The gum is bleeding.	**Tannkjøttet blør.**	**tahn**khurtter blurr

Dentures

I've broken this denture.	**Jeg har brukket dette gebisset.**	yay haar **brokk**ert **deht**ter geh**biss**er
Can you repair this denture?	**Kan De reparere dette gebisset?**	kahn dee rehpah**ray**rer **deht**ter geh**biss**er
What's it going to cost?	**Hva vil det koste?**	vah vil day **koss**ter
When will it be ready?	**Når er det ferdig?**	nawr ær day **fæ'**di

Optician

I've broken my glasses.	Jeg har knust brillene mine.	yay haar knewsst brillerner meener
Can you repair them for me?	Kan De reparere dem for meg?	kahn dee rehpahrayrer dehm for may
When will they be ready?	Når vil de være ferdige?	nawr vil dee vaarer faa'deeer
Can you change the lenses?	Kan De skifte glassene?	kahn dee shifter glahsserner
I want tinted lenses.	Jeg vil ha farget glass.	yay vil haa fahrgert glahss
I've lost one of my contact lenses.	Jeg har mistet en av kontaktlinsene mine.	yay haar misstert ayn ahv koontahktlinsserner meener
I'd like to buy a pair of sun-glasses.	Jeg vil gjerne kjøpe et par sol-briller.	yay vil yaa'ner khurper eht paar sool-brillerr
How much do I owe you?	Hvor mye skylder jeg Dem?	voor mewer shewllerr yay dehm
Do I pay you now or will you send me your bill?	Skal jeg betale nå, eller vil De sende meg regningen?	skahl yay bertaaler naw, ehllerr vil dee sehnner may rayningen

OPTICIAN

Keeping fit

If you want to keep fit while you're away from home, your hotel or local tourist office can help you find a gymnasium.

Where can I find a...?	Hvor finnes...?	voor finners
massage parlour	et massasje-institutt	eht mahsaasher-institewt
physiotherapist	en fysioterapeut	ehn fewssiootehrahpoyt
sauna	en badstue	ehn baadstew
solarium	et solarium	eht soolaareeewm
Turkish bath	et tyrkisk bad	eht tewrkissk baad
Where can I find a gymnasium. I want to work out.	Hvor finnes en gymnastikksal? Jeg trenger mosjon.	voor finners ehn gewmnahsstiksaal? yay trehngerr mooshoon

FOR NUMBERS, see page 175

Reference section

Where do you come from?

Africa	**Afrika**	aafrikkah
Asia	**Asia**	aassiah
Australia	**Australia**	owstraaliah
China	**Kina**	kheenah
Denmark	**Danmark**	dahnmahrk
England	**England**	ehnglahn
Europe	**Europa**	owrōōpah
Finland	**Finland**	finlahn
France	**Frankrike**	frahnkreeker
Germany	**Tyskland**	tewsklahn
Great Britain	**Storbritannia**	stōōrbrittahnyah
India	**India**	indyah
Ireland	**Irland**	eerlan
Japan	**Japan**	yāāpahn
New Zealand	**New Zealand**	nyoo sāylahn
North America	**Nord-Amerika**	nōōr-ahmāyrikkah
Norway	**Norge**	norgger
Scandinavia	**Skandinavia**	skahndinaavyah
Scotland	**Skottland**	skotlahn
South Africa	**Sør-Afrika**	sūrr-aafrikkah
South America	**Sør-Amerika**	sūrr-ahmāyrikkah
Sweden	**Sverige**	sværyeh
USA	**USA**	ēwehssaa
USSR	**Sovjetsamveldet**	sovyehtssahmvehlder
Wales	**Wales**	waylss

And some important Norwegian cities and places...

Arendal	aarerndaal	**Kristiansand**	kristyahnsahn
Bergen	bærgern	**Kristiansund**	kristyahnsewn
Bodø	bōōdūr	**Lillehammer**	lillerhahmmerr
Fagernes	faager'nāyss	**Narvik**	nahrveek
Geilo	yayloo	**Oslo**	oossloo
Gol	gōōl	**Stavanger**	stahvahngerr
Gudbrandsdalen	gewdbrahnss-	**Tjøme**	khūrmer
	daalern	**Tromsø**	troomssūr
Hamar	haamahr	**Trondheim**	tronhaym
Kautokeino	kowtookaynoo	**Tønsberg**	turnssbehrg
Kongsberg	kongssbærg	**Vadsø**	vahdssūr
Kragerø	kraaggehrūr	**Vardø**	vahrdūr

Numbers

0	**null**	newl
1	**en**	āyn
2	**to**	tōo
3	**tre**	trāy
4	**fire**	feerer
5	**fem**	fehm
6	**seks**	sehks
7	**sju**	shēw
8	**åtte**	otter
9	**ni**	nee
10	**ti**	tee
11	**elleve**	ehllver
12	**tolv**	tol
13	**tretten**	trehttern
14	**fjorten**	fyoo'tern
15	**femten**	fehmtern
16	**seksten**	saysstern
17	**sytten**	sewttern
18	**atten**	ahttern
19	**nitten**	nittern
20	**tjue**	khēwer
21	**tjueen**	khēwer-āyn
22	**tjueto**	khēwer-tōo
23	**tjuetre**	khēwer-trāy
24	**tjuefire**	khēwer-feerer
25	**tjuefem**	khēwer-fehm
26	**tjueseks**	khēwer-sehks
27	**tjuesju**	khēwer-shēw
28	**tjueåtte**	khēwer-otter
29	**tjueni**	khēwer-nee
30	**tretti**	trehttee
31	**trettien**	trehttee-āyn
32	**trettito**	trehttee-tōo
33	**trettitre**	trehttee-trāy
40	**førti**	fur'tee
41	**førtien**	fur'tee-āyn
42	**førtito**	fur'tee-tōo
43	**førtitre**	fur'tee-trāy
50	**femti**	fehmtee
51	**femtien**	fehmtee-āyn
52	**femtito**	fehmtee-tōo
53	**femtitre**	fehmtee-trāy
60	**seksti**	sehkstee
61	**sekstien**	sehkstee-āyn
62	**sekstito**	sehkstee-tōo

63	sekstitre	sehkstee-trāy
70	sytti	sewttee
71	syttien	sewttee-āyn
72	syttito	sewttee-tōō
73	syttitre	sewttee-trāy
80	åtti	ottee
81	åttien	ottee-āyn
82	åttito	ottee-tōō
83	åttitre	ottee-trāy
90	nitti	nittee
91	nittien	nittee-āyn
92	nittito	nittee-tōō
93	nittitre	nittee-trāy
100	hundre	hewndreh
101	hundreogen	hewndreh-o-āyn
102	hundreogto	hewndreh-o-tōō
110	hundreogti	hewndreh-o-tee
120	hundreogtjue	hewndreh-o-khēwer
130	hundreogtretti	hewndreh-o-trehttee
140	hundreogførti	hewndreh-o-fur'tee
150	hundreogfemti	hewndreh-o-fehmtee
160	hundreogseksti	hewndreh-o-sehkstee
170	hundreogsytti	hewndreh-o-sewrttee
180	hundreogåtti	hewndreh-o-ottee
190	hundreognitti	hewndreh-o-nittee
200	to hundre	tōō hewndreh
300	tre hundre	trāy hewndreh
400	fire hundre	feerer hewndreh
500	fem hundre	fehm hewndreh
600	seks hundre	sehks hewndreh
700	sju hundre	shēw hewndreh
800	åtte hundre	otter hewndreh
900	ni hundre	nee hewndreh
1000	tusen	tēwssern
1100	et tusen et hundre	eht tēwssern eht hewndreh
1200	et tusen to hundre	eht tēwssern tōō hewndreh
2000	to tusen	tōō tēwssern
5000	fem tusen	fehm tēwssern
10,000	ti tusen	tee tēwssern
50,000	femti tusen	fehmtee tēwssern
100,000	hundre tusen	hewndreh tēwssern
1,000,000	en million	āyn millyōōn
1,000,000,000	en milliard	āyn millyahrd

first	**første**	furshter
second	**andre**	ahndrer
third	**tredje**	trāydyer
fourth	**fjerde**	fyǣrer
fifth	**femte**	fehmter
sixth	**sjette**	shehtter
seventh	**sjuende**	shǣwernder
eighth	**åttende**	otternder
ninth	**niende**	neeernder
tenth	**tiende**	teeernder
once	**en gang**	ehn gahng
twice	**to ganger**	tōō gahngerr
three times	**tre ganger**	trāy gahngerr
a half	**en halv**	ehn hahl
half of...	**halvparten**	hahlpahrtern
half a...	**en halv**	ehn hahl
a quarter	**en kvart**	ehn kvah't
three-quarters	**tre fjerdedeler**	trāy fyǣrerdāylerr
a third	**en tredjedel**	ehn trehdyerdāyl
two-thirds	**to tredjedeler**	tōō trehdyerdāylerr
a pair of	**et par**	eht paar
a dozen	**et dusin**	eht dewsseen
1982	**nitten åttito**	nittern ottee-tōō
1983	**nitten åttitre**	nittern ottee-trāy
1984	**nitten åttifire**	nittern ottee-feerer
1985	**nitten åttifem**	nittern ottee-fehm

Time

kvart over tolv
(kvah't **aw**verr
tol)

ti på halv to
(tee paw hahl tōō)

fem på halv tre
(fehm paw hahl
trāy)

halv fire
(hahl **feerer**)

fem over halv fem
(fehm **aw**verr hahl
fehm)

ti over halv seks
(tee **aw**verr hahl
sehks)

kvart på sju
(kvah't paw shēw)

ti på åtte
(tee paw **otter**)

fem på ni
(fehm paw nee)

ti
(tee)

fem over elleve
(fehm **aw**verr
ehllver)

ti over tolv
(tee **aw**verr tol)

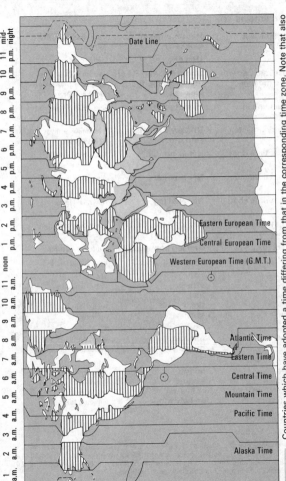

Countries which have adopted a time differing from that in the corresponding time zone. Note that also in the USSR, official time is one hour ahead of the time in each corresponding time zone. In summer, numerous countries advance time one hour ahead of standard time.

Date Line

1 a.m. 2 a.m. 3 a.m. 4 a.m. 5 a.m. 6 a.m. 7 a.m. 8 a.m. 9 a.m. 10 a.m. 11 a.m. noon 1 p.m. 2 p.m. 3 p.m. 4 p.m. 5 p.m. 6 p.m. 7 p.m. 8 p.m. 9 p.m. 10 p.m. 11 p.m. mid-night

Eastern European Time
Central European Time
Western European Time (G.M.T.)

Atlantic Time
Eastern Time
Central Time
Mountain Time
Pacific Time
Alaska Time

What time is it?

What time is it?	**Hvor mange er klokken?**	voor **mahnger** ǣr **klok**kern
It's...	**Den er...**	dehn ær
Excuse me. Can you tell me the time?	**Unnskyld, kan De si meg hvor mange klokken er?**	**ewn**shewl kahn dee see may voor **mahnger klok**kern ǣr
I'll meet you at... tomorrow.	**Vi møtes i morgen kl...**	vee **mūr**ters ee **maw**ern **klok**kern
I'm sorry I'm late.	**Unnskyld at jeg er sent ute.**	**ewn**shewl aht yay ǣr sāynt **ōw**ter
At what time does... open?	**Når åpner...?**	nawr **awp**nerr
At what time does... close?	**Når stenger...?**	nawr **stehn**gerr
At what time should I be there?	**Når skal jeg komme?**	nawr skahl yay **kom**mer
At what time will you be there?	**Når kommer De?**	nawr **kom**merr dee
Can I come...?	**Kan jeg komme...?**	kahn yay **kom**mer
at 8 o'clock/at 2.30	**klokken 8/halv 3 ***	**klok**kern 8/hahl 3
after	**etter**	**eh**terr
afterwards	**etterpå**	**eh**terrpaw
before	**før**	fūrr
early	**tidlig**	**tee**li
in time	**presist**	preh**sseesst**
late	**sent**	saynt
midnight	**midnatt**	**mid**naht
noon	**middag**	**mid**daag
hour	**time**	**tee**mer
minute	**minutt**	mi**newt**
second	**sekund**	seh**kewnn**
quarter of an hour	**et kvarter**	eht kvah'**tāyr**
half an hour	**en halv time**	ehn hahl **tee**mer

*This means, literally, "half to three"; in normal conversation the Norwegians think of the half hour as being half way to the following full hour, not half way after the preceding one, as is our habit. Note that official time uses the 24-hour clock, e.g. 6 p.m. is referred to as 18.00 hrs.

Days

What day is it today?	**Hvilken dag er det i dag?**	vilkern daag **ǣr** daȳ ee daag
Sunday	**søndag**	surndaag
Monday	**mandag**	mahndaag
Tuesday	**tirsdag**	teeshdaag
Wednesday	**onsdag**	oonssdaag
Thursday	**torsdag**	toshdaag
Friday	**fredag**	frāȳdaag
Saturday	**lørdag**	lūr′daag
in the morning	**om morgenen**	om **ma**wernern
during the day	**i løpet av dagen**	ee **lū**rpert ahv **daa**gern
in the afternoon	**om ettermiddagen**	om **eh**terrmidd**daa**gern
in the evening	**om kvelden**	om **kveh**llern
at night	**om natten**	om **nah**ttern
the day before yesterday	**i forgårs**	ee forgawrss
yesterday	**i går**	ee gawr
today	**i dag**	ee daag
tomorrow	**i morgen**	ee **ma**wern
the day after tomorrow	**i overmorgen**	ee **aw**verrmawern
the day before	**dagen før**	**daa**gern fürr
the following day	**dagen etter**	**daa**gern **eh**tterr
two days ago	**for to dager siden**	for tōo **daa**gerr **see**dern
in three days' time	**om en tre dagers tid**	om ehn trāȳ **daa**gersh teed
last week	**forrige uke**	**for**reeer **ēw**ker
next week	**neste uke**	**neh**sster **ēw**ker
for a fortnight (two weeks)	**i fjorten dager**	ee **fyoo′**tern **daa**gerr
birthday	**fødselsdag**	furdss**ser**lssdaag
day	**dag**	daag
day off	**fridag**	**free**daag
holiday	**helligdag**	**heh**lleedaag
holidays	**ferie**	**fāȳ**ryer
month	**måned**	**maw**nerd
school holidays	**skoleferie**	**skōō**lerfāȳryer
vacation	**ferie**	**fāȳ**ryer
week	**uke**	**ēw**ker
weekday	**ukedag**	**ēw**kerdaag
working day	**arbeidsdag**	**ahr**baydssdaag

Note: The names of days and months are not capitalized in Norwegian.

Months

January	**januar**	yahnewaar
February	**februar**	fehbrewaar
March	**mars**	mahsh
April	**april**	ahpreel
May	**mai**	maai
June	**juni**	yēwnee
July	**juli**	yēwlee
August	**august**	owgewst
September	**september**	sehptehmberr
October	**oktober**	oktawberr
November	**november**	noovehmberr
December	**desember**	dehssehmberr

since June	**siden juni**	seedern yēwnee
during the month of August	**i løpet av august måned**	ee lūrpert ahv owgewst mawnerd
last month	**forrige måned**	forreeer mawnerd
next month	**neste måned**	nehsster mawnerd
the month before	**måneden før**	mawnehdern fūrr
the following month	**måneden etter**	mawnehdern ehtterr
July 1	**første juli**	furshter yēwlee
March 17	**syttende mars**	sewtterner mahsh

Letter headings are written thus:

Oslo, August 17, 19..   **Oslo, 17. august 19..**

Bergen, July 1, 19..   **Bergen, 1. juli 19..**

Seasons

spring	**vår**	vawr
summer	**sommer**	sommerr
autumn	**høst**	hursst
winter	**vinter**	vinterr

in spring	**om våren**	om vawrern
during the summer	**om sommeren**	om sommerrern
last autumn	**forrige høst**	forreeer hursst
next winter	**neste vinter**	nehsster vinterr

Public holidays

January 1, New Year's Day	**Nyttår**	newttawr
May 1, Labour Day	**Arbeidets dag**	aar**bay**dertss daag
May 17, Constitution Day	**Nasjonaldagen**	nashoo**naal**daagern
December 25, Christmas Day	**Første juledag**	furshter y͞ewlerdaag
December 26, St. Stephen's Day	**Annen juledag**	ahnnern y͞ewlerdaag

Movable dates:

Maundy Thursday	**Skjærtorsdag**	shǣr**tosh**daag
Good Friday	**Langfredag**	lahng**frāy**daag
Easter Monday	**Annen påskedag**	ahnnern **paws**skerdaag
Ascension Day	**Kristi himmelfarts-dag**	krisstee **him**merlfahrtss-daag
Whit Monday	**Annen pinsedag**	ahnnern **pins**sedaag

Seasonal temperatures

Here are the average monthly temperatures in centigrade and Fahrenheit for some Norwegian cities:

	Oslo	Bergen	Bodø
January	− 6 °C (21 °F)	0 °C (32 °F)	0 °C (31 °F)
April	4 °C (40 °F)	5 °C (42 °F)	6 °C (43 °F)
July	18 °C (65 °F)	15 °C (59 °F)	15 °C (59 °F)
October	6 °C (44 °F)	8 °C (47 °F)	5 °C (41 °F)

Common abbreviations

A/S	aksjeselskap	Ltd., Inc.
bl.a.	blant annet	among other things, *inter al.*
d.	død	died
d.v.s.	det vil si	that is to say, i.e.
EF	Det Europeiske Fellesskap	European Economic Community (Common Market)
e.Kr.	etter Kristi fødsel	A.D.
f.	født	born
f.eks.	for eksempel	for instance, e.g.
fj.	fjord	fjord
f.Kr.	før Kristi fødsel	B.C.
FN	Forente Nasjoner	United Nations
frk.	frøken	Miss
...gt.	gate	street
hr.	herr	Mr.
innb.	innbyggere	inhabitants
KFUK	Kristelig Forening for Unge Kvinner	Y.W.C.A.
KFUM	Kristelig Forening for Unge Menn	Y.M.C.A.
kl.	klokken	o'clock
KNA	Kongelig Norsk Automobil-klub	Royal Norwegian Automobile Club
kr.	krone(r)	crown(s)
moms	merverdiavgift	value added tax
NAF	Norges Automobil-Forbund	Norwegian Automobile Association
NMK	Norsk Motor Klubb	Norwegian Motor Club
nr.	nummer	number
NRK	Norsk Rikskringkasting	Norwegian Broadcasting Service
NSB	Norges Statsbaner	Norwegian State Railways
NTB	Norsk Telegrambyrå	Norwegian News Bureau
NUH	Norske Ungdomsherberger	Norwegian Youth Hostels Association
osv.	og så videre	etc.
tlf.	telefon	telephone
...vn	veien, vegen	road

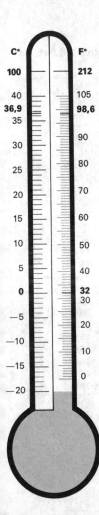

Conversion tables

To change centimetres into inches, multiply by .39.

To change inches into centimetres, multiply by 2.54.

Centimeters and inches

	in.	feet	yards
1 mm	0,039	0,003	0,001
1 cm	0,39	0,03	0,01
1 dm	3,94	0,32	0,10
1 m	39,40	3,28	1,09

	mm	cm	m
1 in.	25,4	2,54	0,025
1 ft.	304,8	30,48	0,304
1 yd.	914,4	91,44	0,914

(32 metres = 35 yards)

Temperature

To convert Centigrade into degrees Fahrenheit, multiply Centigrade by 1.8 and add 32.

To convert degrees Fahrenheit into Centigrade, subtract 32 from Fahrenheit and divide by 1.8.

Metres and feet

The figure in the middle stands for both metres and feet, e.g.
1 metre = 3.281 ft. and 1 foot = 0.30 m.

Metres		Feet
0.30	1	3.281
0.61	2	6.563
0.91	3	9.843
1.22	4	13.124
1.52	5	16.403
1.83	6	19.686
2.13	7	22.967
2.44	8	26.248
2.74	9	29.529
3.05	10	32.810
3.35	11	36.091
3.66	12	39.372
3.96	13	42.635
4.27	14	45.934
4.57	15	49.215
4.88	16	52.496
5.18	17	55.777
5.49	18	59.058
5.79	19	62.339
6.10	20	65.620
7.62	25	82.023
15.24	50	164.046
22.86	75	246.069
30.48	100	328.092

Other conversion charts

For	see page
Clothing sizes	115
Currency converter	136
Distance (miles-kilometres)	144
Fluid measures	143
Tire pressure	143

REFERENCE SECTION

Weight conversion

The figure in the middle stands for both kilograms and pounds, e.g. 1 kilogram = 2.20 lbs. and 1 lb. = 0.45 kilograms.

Kilograms (kg.)		Avoirdupois pounds
0.45	1	2.205
0.90	2	4.405
1.35	3	6.614
1.80	4	8.818
2.25	5	11.023
2.70	6	13.227
3.15	7	15.432
3.60	8	17.636
4.05	9	19.840
4.50	10	22.045
6.75	15	33.068
9.00	20	44.889
11.25	25	55.113
22.50	50	110.225
33.75	75	165.338
45.00	100	220.450

NORTH
NORD
(noor)

WEST
VEST
(vehsst)

EAST
ØST
(ursst)

SOUTH
SØR
(surr)

REFERENCE SECTION

What does that sign mean?

You're sure to encounter some of these signs or notices on your trip.

REFERENCE SECTION

Damer	Ladies
Fare	Danger
...forbudt	...forbidden
Forsiktig	Caution
Forsiktig, trapp	Mind the step
Gratis adgang	Admission free
Heis	Lift (elevator)
Herrer	Gentlemen
Ikke rør	Do not touch
Informasjon	Information
Ingen adgang	No entrance
Ingen overtredelse	No trespassing
Inngang	Entrance
Kald	Cold
Kasse	Cashier's
Kom rett inn	Enter without knocking
Ledig	Vacant
Livsfarlig	Danger of Death
Nødutgang	Emergency exit
Vokt Dem for hunden	Beware of the dog
Privat	Private
Privat vei	Private road
Reservert	Reserved
Røyking forbudt	No smoking
Stengt	Closed
Sykkelsti	Cycle path
Til leie	To let, for hire
Til salgs	For sale
Trekk	Pull
Trykk	Push
Utgang	Exit
Utsalg	Sales
Utsolgt	Sold out
Varm	Hot
Vennligst ring	Please ring
Vennligst vent	Please wait

Emergency

By the time the emergency is upon you it's too late to turn to this page to find the Norwegian for "I'll scream if you...". So have a look at this short list beforehand—and, if you want to be on the safe side, learn the expressions shown in capitals.

Be quick	Skynd Dem	shewn dehm
Call the police	Ring politiet	ring pooliteeer
CAREFUL	FORSIKTIG	foshikti
Come here	Kom hit	kom heet
Come in	Kom inn	kom inn
Danger	Fare	faarer
Fire	Brann	brahn
Gas	Gass	gahss
Get a doctor	Få tak i lege	faw taak ee layger
Go away	Gå vekk	gaw vehk
HELP	HJELP	yehlp
Get help quickly	Få tak i hjelp fort	faw taak ee yehlp foo't
I'm ill	Jeg er dårlig	yay ær daw'li
I'm lost	Jeg har gått meg bort	yay haar got may boo't
I've lost my...	Jeg har mistet min...	yay haar misstert meen
Keep your hands to yourself	Fingrene fra fatet	fingrerner fraa fahter
Leave me alone	La meg være	laa may værer
Lie down	Ligg ned	lig nay
Listen	Hør her	hurr hær
Listen to me	Hør på meg	hurr paw may
Look	se	say
LOOK OUT	SE OPP	say op
POLICE	POLITI	poolitee
Quick	Fort	foo't
STOP	STOPP	stop
Stop here	Stopp her	stop hær
Stop that man	Stopp den mannen	stop dehn mahnnern
Stop thief	Stopp tyven	stop tewvern
Stop or I'll scream	Stopp, ellers skriker jeg	stop ehllerrss skreekerr yay

FOR CAR ACCIDENTS, see page 150

190

Index

Abbreviations	184
Arrival	22
Baggage	24
Bank	25, 134
Basic expressions	16
Beach	87
Body, parts of	163
Breakfast	34
Bus	73
Camping	90
equipment	106
Car	142
accidents	150
breakdown	151
documents	146
filling station	142
parts	155
rental	26
repair	152
speed limits	148
Church services	79
Cinema	80
Clothes	112
Colours	113
Complaints	35, 60
Concerts	82
Countries	174
Customs control	23, 146
Dancing	84
Dating	95
Days	181
Dentist	172
Directions	25, 144
Doctor	162
Drinks	61
Dry cleaning	126
Eating out	38
appetizers	44
cheese	56
dessert	58
drinks	61
egg dishes	46
fish and seafood	49
fruit	57
game and fowl	53
koldtbord	46
meat	51
Norwegian specialities	45, 52, 53
salads	45
sandwiches	45
sauces	55
snacks	64
soups	47
vegetables	54
Electrical appliances	119
Emergency	189
Friends	93
Gambling	85
Games	84
Grammar	7
Hairdressing	121
Hotel	28
breakfast	34
checking in	29
checking out	37
difficulties	35
registration	32
reservation	25
service	33
Introductions	93
Invitations	95

Landmarks	91
Laundry	126
Lost property	72
Materials (clothes)	113
Meal times	39
Measurements	
fluids	143
km/miles	144
metric	186
sizes (clothing)	115
temperature	185
tire pressure	143
weight	186
Medical section	162
Money	25, 134
Months	182
Movies	80
Music	120
Nightclubs	83
Numbers	175
Optician	173
Passport control	22
Porters	24, 71
Post-office	137
Pronunciation	12
Public holidays	183
Reference section	174
Relaxing	80
Restaurants	38
Roads	147
Road signs	
Norwegian	149
international	160
Seasons	182
Shopping guide	97
barber's	121

bookshop	104
camping	106
chemist's	108
clothing	112
drugstore	108
electrical appliances	119
hairdresser's	121
jeweller's	123
laundry	126
news-stand	104
pharmacy	108
photography	127
provisions	130
records	120
shoes	116
shops, list of	98
souvenirs	132
stationer's	104
tobacconist's	133
toiletry	110
Sightseeing	75
Signs and notices	188
Sports	86
Taxis	27
Telegrams	138
Telephone	139
Temperature	183, 185
Theatre	80
Time	178
Travel	65
boat	74
bus	73
car	142
plane	65
tickets	69
train	66
underground (subway)	72
Weather	94
Winter sports	89

Quick reference page

Here are some phrases and expressions which you'll probably need most frequently on your trip:

Please.	**Vær så snill.**	vǣr saw snil
Thank you.	**Takk.**	tahk
Yes/No.	**Ja/Nei.**	yah/nay
Excuse me.	**Unnskyld.**	ewnshewl
Waiter, please.	**Kelner!**	kehlnerr
How much is that?	**Hva koster det?**	vah **koss**terr dāy
Where are the toilets?	**Hvor er toalettene?**	voor ǣr tooah**leht**terner

Toaletter	
MENN (mehn)	KVINNER (kvinnerr)

Could you tell me...?	**Kan De si meg...?**	kahn dee see may
where/when/why	**hvor/når/hvorfor**	voor/nawr/**voor**for
Help me, please.	**Vær så snill å hjelpe meg.**	vǣr saw snil aw **yehl**per may
What time is it?	**Hvor mange er klokken?**	voor **mahng**er ǣr klokkern
one/first	**en/første**	āyn/**fursh**ter
two/second	**to/andre**	tōō/**ahn**drer
three/third	**tre/tredje**	trāy/**trāy**dyer
What does this mean?	**Hva betyr dette?**	vah ber**tēwr deht**ter
I don't understand.	**Jeg forstår ikke...**	yay fo**shtawr ik**ker
Do you speak English?	**Snakker De engelsk?**	**snahk**kerr dee **ehn**gerlsk